For **Bernardine Evaristo** style is about a refusal to be stereotyped. **Jilly Cooper** and **AJ Tracey** appreciate retail therapy. **Sienna Miller** misses the freedom of a less self-conscious age. For **Davina McCall**, an outfit begins with underwear; for **Sophie Dahl** it's not complete without scent. Clothes allow **Susie Cave** to hide and **Charlotte Tilbury** to feel empowered.

With over sixty pieces on everything from thrifting to modesty dressing, drag to vintage sportswear, *Style and Substance* is a gloriously eclectic celebration of self-expression.

STYLE AND SUBSTANCE

Why What We Wear Matters

EDITED BY **BAY GARNETT**

JOHN MURRAY

First published in Great Britain in 2023 by John Murray (Publishers)

I

Copyright © Bay Garnett 2023

All pieces © Bay Garnett, with the exception of those listed on page 231
which constitute an extension of this copyright page.

Cover and internal illustrations © 2023 Rosie McGuinness

A CIP catalogue record for this title is available from the British Library

Hardback ISBN 978 1 399 81244 3
Trade Paperback ISBN 978 1 399 81525 3
ebook ISBN 978 1 399 81246 7

Typeset in Mrs Eaves by Palimpsest Book Production Limited, Falkirk, Stirlingshire

Printed and bound in Italy by L.E.G.O. SpA

John Murray policy is to use papers that are natural, renewable
and recyclable products and made from wood grown in sustainable forests.
The logging and manufacturing processes are expected to conform
to the environmental regulations of the country of origin.

Carmelite House
50 Victoria Embankment
London EC4Y 0DZ

www.johnmurraypress.co.uk

John Murray Press, part of Hodder & Stoughton Limited
An Hachette UK company

To my mother, Polly Devlin

CONTENTS

PART 3
STYLE TRIBES

PART 4
COLOUR

PART 5
DRESSING UP

'My dress fitted perfectly and everyone said
that I looked like a sunbeam in it.'

I Know Why the Caged Bird Sings

INTRODUCTION

IN 1998 I WAS IN New York. It was a sunny day and I'd taken the N train from Manhattan to the big Salvation Army in Steinway, Astoria in Queens. Ben E. King was playing loudly on the radio while all kinds of people rummaged through the huge store looking for a stylish bargain, or just sitting on the sofas, happy to have a place to rest. I remember it as one of the happiest days of my life. Here I was, alone, sun shining, doing what I loved to do.

I was working as an assistant at a photographic agency but I spent every lunch break and weekend seeking out new thrift stores and returning to my favourites. Whenever I turned up to meet friends, I was always hauling a black bin bag full of other people's old clothes over one shoulder. Old clothes gave me new ideas. I loved imagining who would have worn the clothes hanging up and thinking about how I might borrow the glamour or rebellion of a previous era. The purple and black zebra tight V-neck was pure Joan Jett. I found a perfect early eighties tobacco-coloured cashmere Calvin Klein coat that was totally a young Brooke Shields. I'd put on a preppy men's shirt and could imagine I was Lauren Hutton; picking up a polka dot YSL blouse put me in a mind of Catherine Deneuve. Clothes gave me a confidence in myself as a storyteller that I'd never had at school.

When the dazzlingly stylish Kira Jolliffe, a friend of my older sister, said 'I am going to start a fanzine called *Cheap Date* about second-hand clothes, c'mon board!' my hobby became a part-time job. One of my first projects was interviewing and photographing Chloë Sevigny. I'd seen her at a party wearing patent high pumps on which she'd tied a red velvet ribbon around the arch in a bow and I had been fixated by this thoughtful detail. When she opened the door of her apartment in Gramercy Park,

1

she was wearing a thrifted little yellow bathing suit with a lace collar. She was amazing. I took her picture with my point and shoot camera and she was our *Cheap Date* centrefold. It's still one of my favourite photos.

Marlon Richards was the Art Director and it was through him that I met his mother, Anita Pallenberg. She was standing by the office window, smoking a cigarette and wearing huge shades, a striped roll neck and tough Maharishi trousers. I was suitably intimidated.

When I moved back to London, I would go to Anita's house in Chelsea, look through her wardrobe and lie on the early Vivienne Westwood velvet and leopard cushions piled on her sofa, while she told me about the stories behind her clothes. The thrift shops around World's End in Chelsea were brilliant – still are. They were the only shops we ever went to. Boy, did she have an eye! She would find amazing stuff everywhere – sneaking off around a corner and then emerging triumphant, holding her trophy in the air, grinning ear to ear. She had the most refined taste but loved a bargain and we delighted in giving each other things that we'd found and knew the other would love.

For the last few issues of *Cheap Date* we'd created fake ads riffing off the styling and typefaces the big houses were using for their advertising but using clothes we'd found. The idea was to make people do a double take and rethink their ideas about the difference between high fashion and thrift stores. While at first glance, it might have looked like Yves Saint Laurent, the model was wearing Salvation Army. Calvin Klein became Cancer Care, Burberry was Borrowed, Cartier named Castoff, Bulgari morphed into Budget – you get the idea. What was brilliant was that thanks to the generosity of models and photographers (Craig McDean and Glen Luchford), our images were shot and retouched (thank you, Pascal Dangin) by the same people who were creating the luxury labels' images. Albeit ours were done in thirty minutes, which meant there wasn't time to steam the outfits I pulled out of my bin bag.

Cheap Date led to a call from Alexandra Shulman. I remember thinking 'what do I wear to meet the editor of *Vogue*?' and deciding on a pair of huge furry Yeti boots. The first idea I pitched was a shoot using the clothes that Anita and I had accumulated from our second-hand and charity shops trawls. Together Anita and I pulled together our collection. Anita insisted we include her white fake fur monkey jacket (way before fake fur was a thing), I was obsessed with a banana-print top, little shorts, a weave belt and Kira's old cowboy boots. Juergen Teller shot the story and Kate Moss was, of course, the perfect model. She looked so good in the gold sequin jacket I'd found for seven dollars in the Salvation Army store on Spring Street that I gave it to her.

That *Vogue* shoot, the first time a fashion magazine did a story using old clothes, was twenty years ago. Last year I worked with Oxfam on curating the show that opened London Fashion Week. It feels like the conversation around second-hand — the importance of sustainability in fashion as well as the creative joy of curating an original look — has come a long way.

Editing this book has been like putting a fashion show or magazine story together — but with a lot more words. It is, I hope, richly textured and full of the delight that comes with finding something unexpected. With enormous thanks to the incredibly stylish and inspiring people who have opened their hearts, and wardrobes, to be part of this book, I hope it inspires you to appreciate the many ways clothes can let us feel who we most want to be.

Bay Garnett

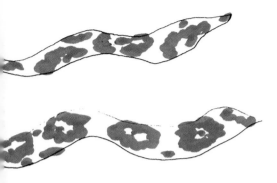

PART 1

FREEDOM

'Vain trifles as they seem,
clothes have, they say, more important
offices than to keep us warm.
They change our view of the world
and the world's view of us.'

VIRGINIA WOOLF, *Orlando*

'I do like underwear, but not all the time.
Sometimes you gotta let the girls go free.'

DEBBIE HARRY

BERNARDINE EVARISTO
on Making a Statement

This piece from the first Black woman to win the Booker Prize for her novel *Girl, Woman, Other* (2019), first appeared on 'Net-a-Porter' in 2020.

AS A CHILD, I WAS called a 'tomboy' due to my rumbustious energy, tendency towards scruffiness and propensity for climbing trees, instead of comporting myself with ladylike decorum. It's such sexist nonsense, of course, and it's astonishing that these gender proscriptions are still imposed on children today. Eventually, my spirited younger self morphed into a teenager who wore patched-up jeans, hippy sandals (aka 'Jesus creepers') and shape-less sweaters. It was the beginning of my conscious rebellion against gender expectations. I did once succumb to wearing a pair of platforms but, when I fell over and almost snapped my ankle, I swore never to wear heels again.

By my early twenties, I was deeply politicized and raging against the machine. I sported baggy old coats, men's trousers, knitted waistcoats, red baseball boots, and my hair was either in a buzz cut or exploding with spiky dreadlocks. I was often mistaken for a boy, which annoyed me because I wanted my image to reflect my feminist theatre-maker identity as a woman, in spite of my attire. I was also rejecting the tacit expectation that, as a black woman in 1980s Britain, I should try to be as unnoticeable as possible; to mitigate my darker skin through conformist clothing.

In my novel *Girl, Woman, Other*, the characters of Amma and Dominique (lesbian feminists who run a black and Asian women's theatre company) best illustrate my younger countercultural sartorial sensibility, as they similarly strive to break free from society's shackles. Conversely, Shirley, their schoolteacher contemporary, straightens her hair and clads herself in understated 'feminine' clothes, hoping to be regarded as an unassailable paragon of respectability. A generation later, Carole, a working-class girl of Nigerian parentage, adopts the same modus operandi. Her meticulously perfected grooming represents the straitjacketing of her personality in order to succeed in the corporate world and the elevated social circles of her aspiration. In one sense, these are two extremes of black British womanhood. Amma and Dominique's 'warrior wear' style signals their readiness to do battle with an unequal society, as it did for me, unaccepting of the secondary status imposed on me as a woman of color in a majority-white society.

By the end of the 1980s, I was beginning to change. The fire that fuelled my fury at an exclusionary society did not stop burning, but instead it was transmuted from anger into an energy that has kept me going ever since. I left theatre behind and worked in arts management to support my writing career. At one stage, I began to dress as if I worked in an office — according to a friend who was appalled at my adoption of skirts, blouses, nylon tights and brogues. She chose to ignore the fact that the skirts were funky, the tights a bright tartan, and my brogues an electric blue. At this stage, I wanted to write books, with no idea if it would work out. It was a leap of faith motivated by the desire for my stories to be heard in this society. And, over the years, I felt it was my duty to never give up because, if so, how could I justifiably complain about our marginalization as women of color?

By the noughties, society was changing around me, too. We were becoming more integrated in Britain, although the flames of feminism were on the back burner and would remain so until recently. It was really only the #MeToo movement that precipitated a paradigm shift in our culture that saw young women, in particular, claiming and defining feminism for a new generation. Once that happened, I began to see young black women with a similar look to my younger self, with their shaved heads, gender-disrupting clothes, heavy laced boots and edgy attitudes. The big difference is that, these days, they are to be found modelling in the fashion pages of magazines.

In spite of my early sartorial androgyny, I feel comfortable with the gender I was assigned at birth and have never felt the need to transition to an alternative, but I understand why some people want to dispense with the idea of gender binaries altogether, along with its restricting and reductive codes and rules.

In the novel, Megan, one of my twelve protagonists, transitions from being a woman to identifying as non-binary, choosing the name of Morgan, and adopting the personal pronoun 'they'. Morgan undergoes a voluntary mastectomy, wears non-binary clothes and perplexes people who want to categorize them as either male or female. Their new identity is considered a radical act in a society steeped in restrictive gender binaries that are inculcated in us pre-birth, indeed, as soon as our parents start buying blue baby clothes for a boy and pink for a girl.

At different stages in my life, I have been a flamboyant dresser, just as I am a flamboyant writer, a literary experimentalist who treasures individuality. When I go hunting for clothes, I scan shops for the brightest, most distinctive colors. A shirt of bright pink, lemon and orange swirls? Lovely! This I will mismatch with a multicolored African-print headscarf. **Beige is anathema to me. Black depresses me if I don't break it up with a startlingly loud color.** Whenever I am forced to travel in the rush hour, I am amazed at how even my, say, bright orange scarf stands out amid the overwhelmingly dark clothes. Women of color are hyper-visible in some situations, on account of our darker skin making us stand out, and simultaneously invisible, when we don't have a platform from which to speak out. **My style is a visual statement and representation of myself as a woman in the arts who is a creative thinker.** It signifies that I cannot be stereotyped, controlled or silenced.

DAVID BOWIE
on Ziggy

A sensational style chameleon, David Bowie invented
characters and pioneered looks. In a programme on
BBC Radio I in 1993, he talked about the evolution
of Ziggy Stardust.

MOST OF THE LOOK FOR Ziggy was basically from the Kubrick
film *Clockwork Orange*. I thought the jumpsuits in that movie were
just wonderful. I liked the malicious, malevolent, viscous quality
of those four guys, although the aspects of violence themselves
didn't turn me on particularly. I wanted to put another spin on
that, so I went to Liberty's (probably a shop on Tottenham Court
Road but Liberty sounds better). I picked out these very florid,
bright quilted kind of materials which took the edge off the
violence of those suits but retained that type of terrorist 'we-are-
ready-for-action' kind of look. And I borrowed the wrestling
boots with laces – but I changed their colour and made them
greens and blues. So that was the basic look but instead of just
having one eyelash I went the whole hog and had two eyelashes.

Even the inset photographs of the inside sleeve for *Ziggy* owed
a lot to the Malcolm McDowell look from the *Clockwork Orange*
poster – the sort of sinister-looking photograph somewhere
between a beetle – not a *Beatle* person, but a real beetle – and
violence. Burgess' idea of having this phoney-speak thing – that
drew on Russian words and put them into the English language,
and twisted old Shakespearean words around – fitted in perfectly
with what I was trying to do in creating this fake world. **It was
like trying to anticipate a society that hadn't happened.**

HARRIS REED
on Fluidity

Harris is half-British, half-American and all style. His distinctive creations are designed to spark conversations about liberation, identity and social justice, and caught the eye of celebrities when he was barely out of his teens. He's created his own demi-couture clothing brand, worked on campaigns for Gucci and gender fluid make-up for Mac. He sometimes wears his waist-length auburn hair in two plaits.

I DRESS TO DREAM AND I design clothes for people to dream in, but my style is not just otherworldly; it's also very specific. At Central Saint Martins I became obsessed with history, and Victorian and Edwardian styles in particular. I fell in love with the opulence of the billowing fabrics, the lace and trimmings. I feel romantic about those eras.

Romanticism for me is dark, sultry and Gothic. I think we've lost some of the romanticism of everyday life now that we all live online and everything must be instantaneous, new and clean. It's harder to design and wear clothes with mystery because we're all so obsessed with novelty, with the latest streetwear brand or micro-trend. It risks feeling a little superficial. I miss the escape into imagination that's inherent in Romanticism. I think we need that in challenging times. It can also be a way to tackle contemporary issues with elegance and depth. Fluidity and sustainability are my two recurring style obsessions, and I like to imbue them both with a touch of Romanticism.

My own style is genderless. I make what I think of as bodyless clothes that can be worn by anybody. Gender fluidity is one form

11

of fluid identity but there are so many more. Fluidity is about adaptation, and fluid thinking allows ideas to flow from one state to another. That's what connects gender fluidity and sustainability for me.

I tried to bring all this together when I designed a collection for Oxfam using wedding dresses that had been donated to their stores. I love to wear and use found objects and there was something magical about taking these dresses that had been made for a single day, and turning them into clothes that could be worn over and over, by anybody who loved them. When I did the collection I was just starting out. I loved rich fabrics with beading and embellishment and embroidery but I couldn't afford to buy them new. My intention was to make luxe accessible for a broad range of people, including myself. Taking a piece of clothing that some would say had reached the end of its life and transforming it with the power of your appreciation and attention: I think that's a romantic act.

Clothes allow us to pass on love from one person to another, or one generation to another. It's an old-fashioned idea to buy a beautiful jacket or dress, cherish it and eventually pass it on to your son or daughter, but it also feels very contemporary.

Somebody with great style has a bold personality that they allow to speak through their clothes. It's about being authentic, which really just means being specific to you. Rather than buying what magazines tell you to, or what's cool on Insta, you dress for your personality. Being stylish is also about thinking in slightly disjointed ways that leads to mismatched looks. It's putting together a melange of something old and new, borrowed and given. I have this conversation with people a lot. Sometimes I say, 'This is beautiful, but is it you?' Be true. That's the only way.

Style for me has always been about freedom, and has been quite separate from the reality of the physical body. Though I've recently had to start making some concessions to what my body might need, as opposed to what my dreaming mind wants. I've just bought a pair of jeans and some vintage loafers, on my doctor's orders. He basically told me that my back was ruined from wearing platforms all day every day, and I might never be able to have children if I didn't get out of tight pants! So flat shoes and loose trousers are now my look for working in the studio. But when I go out, it's back to heels and tight pants.

The thing is, growing up as a queer person in a very conservative part of the United States, I really had to inhabit my own head in order to convince myself that everything was going to be okay. I got used to living at a remove from my body. I've embraced the power of that. Imaginative freedom, mental freedom, that's what clothes represent to me. So a restricted range of movement or a certain degree of discomfort really doesn't bother me. Clothes are transformative. They allow us to embody who we always wanted to be and who we really are.

It's not always been easy for me to convey these ideas. At university, some of my tutors suggested that I was making costume and I should stop designing menswear. I struggled to explain that this is just my take on daywear. It took Harry Styles to wear my pussy-bow blouse and chiffon-trimmed flares for people to get it. I'm fine with that. Sometimes you have to see something to believe it.

I've been very influenced by theatricality, performance and the idea of clothes as a prop for transformation. The avant-garde choreographer Lindsay Kemp, David Bowie and glam rock have all been inspirational, as has Sally Potter's film *Orlando*. The costumes were so sumptuous and I loved the way the character flowed between genders and different historical periods. That film made me believe in my more out-there, theatrical ideas. Tilda Swinton herself has become a bit of an obsession. She can wear a super femme Chanel gown one evening and razor-sharp tailoring the next. She's fiercely otherworldly. These days I'm also inspired by fifteen-year-olds on TikTok wearing their boy-

or girlfriend's closet, thrifting with so much style and dressing up in found items. I love that high energy and boldness.

My thinking brain tells me the world is not in a good place and fashion is wasteful with raw materials being a leading cause of carbon emissions. So if I'm going to make things, my dreaming brain needs them to be beautiful and true and full of purpose.

The first piece I bought with my own money:

When I was thirteen I bought a pink Lacoste shirt and wore it to school in Arizona. That caused a stir! The first expensive item was a pair of silver platform boots, which I bought just after I made the first collection of tour clothes for Harry Styles. I donated them to the V&A for their menswear exhibition in 2021.

The one piece I'd save if my home was on fire:

A faux-snakeskin and faux-fur Alexander McQueen jacket I bought in a second-hand store in Palm Springs when I was seventeen. It was just before I left the States to move to Britain to study. I felt like Penny Lane in *Almost Famous* when I tried it on. That confidence-giving jolt of power was exactly what I needed as a queer person moving to a new country. My shoulders are bursting through it now but I don't know what I would do without it. It's an emblem of freedom and discovery.

VIRGINIA WOOLF
on Change

Virginia Woolf is one of the most influential modernist writers of the twentieth century. Inspired by her lover and fellow Bloomsbury group member Vita Sackville-West, *Orlando* (1928) follows the remarkable life of its gender-fluid, time-defying titular protagonist.

ORLANDO LOOKED NO MORE. HE dashed downhill. He let himself in at a wicket gate. He tore up the winding staircase. He reached his room. He tossed his stockings to one side of the room, his jerkin to the other. He dipped his head. He scoured his hands. He pared his finger nails. With no more than six inches of looking-glass and a pair of old candles to help him, **he had thrust on crimson breeches, lace collar, waistcoat of taffeta, and shoes with rosettes on them as big as double dahlias in less than ten minutes** by the stable clock. He was ready. He was flushed. He was excited, but he was terribly late.

———

Different though the sexes are, they intermix, in every human being a vacillation from one sex to the other takes place, and often it is only the clothes that keep the male or female likeness, while underneath the sex is the very opposite of what is above.

———

Vain trifles as they seem, clothes have, they say, more important offices than merely to keep us warm. There is much to support the view that **it is clothes that wear us and not we them**; we may make them take the mould of arm or breast but they mould our hearts, our brains, our tongues to their liking.

15

AMROU AL-KADHI
on Discovering Their Drag Aesthetic

Self-described 'professional unicorn' Amrou Al-Kadhi
— aka Glamrou — is a queer British-Iraqi writer, actor,
director and drag artist. The following extracts are from
their Polari prize-winning memoir, *Life as a Unicorn*.

IN THE MARINE WORLD, GENDER fluidity and non-conformism
are the status quo. There are sea slugs called nudibranches that
defy sexual categorisation, containing both female and male repro-
ductive organs, giving and receiving in each sexual encounter, with
kaleidoscopic patterns to rival those of a resplendent drag queen.
Marine snail sea hares are able to change sex at will; cuttlefish can
alter the pigments of their exterior with the sartorial flexibility of
Alexander McQueen, and can disguise themselves as the opposite
gender as a social tool; while a male seahorse is something of an
underwater feminist, sharing the labour of pregnancy by carrying
and 'birthing' the young. This was where I needed to be. I mean,
it just seemed so damn *woke* in the ocean.

———

I went on eBay and ordered myself a pair of heels and a giant
blonde wig (which looked a bit like an electrocuted guinea pig).
I hadn't worked out what my drag aesthetic might be at this point
in my life, but these objects just spoke to me, like glittery queer
Horcruxes that would make me indestructible.

———

Seeing my reflection in drag for the very first time was an uncanny
kind of reunion, an introduction to a person I had always had
inside me, yet had somehow always missed. I recognised the

person in the mirror more than I had ever recognised my own image, experiencing the same fuzzy harmony as when I first gazed into a formless marine aquarium. Again, my gender dysphoria was suddenly appeased, and here in front of me was a true manifestation of my internal self. It was time for everyone to meet her.

One of the things that I've come to find interesting about being in drag, is that once you're dressed and made up, you so rarely *see* yourself in drag (unless your outfit involves some kind of reflective device). As a result, your image belongs more to the people who are viewing you, and you start to perceive yourself in how you are being perceived in the eyes gazing at you. **That night, the eyes of everyone I spoke to seemed bewitched by the confidence of the queen in their presence,** with no knowledge of the sorrowing mess she had been just moments before the doors opened.

Drag is a visual assertion of identity that doesn't rely on words or explanations. When you walk into a room in drag, you immediately take up space. Your stilettos echo and your fabrics billow; the glitter on your eyelids refracts the light, and your every step has heft.

When I created Glamrou, my drag persona, I replaced my long-felt invisibility with ultra visibility, and it told the world that I loved being me. It told the world that I was proud to be queer. It told the world that I was defiantly myself. As Glamrou, I got to live out thought patterns that were the opposite of those that governed the entirety of my day out of drag.

ROBERT HERRICK
on Silk

A supporter of King Charles I, Robert Herrick was a
Cavalier poet. This poem, written in 1648, was one of
several addressed to Julia.

> Whenas in silks my Julia goes,
> Then, then (methinks) how sweetly flows
> That liquefaction of her clothes
>
> Next, when I cast mine eyes, and see
> That brave vibration each way free
> O how that glittering taketh me!

DEBORAH LEVY
on Counterpoints

Deborah Levy, twice shortlisted for the Man Booker Prize, is the author of *Hot Milk* and *Swimming Home*. This excerpt is from *The Cost of Living* (2018), the second book in her critically acclaimed 'living autobiography' trilogy which humorously confronts essential questions about modern womanhood.

WHEN I WASN'T WRITING AND teaching and unpacking boxes, my attention was on mending the blocked pipes under the basin in the bathroom. This involved unscrewing all the parts, placing a bucket under the pipes and not knowing what to do next. I had borrowed a mysterious machine from the cardiologist who lived downstairs. It was like a Hoover except it had wires which were then inserted into the tube. It was early morning and I was wearing what is sometimes called a French postman's jacket over my nightdress. It was not a deliberate decision to wear a blue postman's jacket for a plumbing job, not at all, it just happened to be hanging on the hook in the bathroom and it kept me warm. The clash between the thick utilitarian cotton of the jacket and the flimsy nightdress seemed to sum everything up for me, but I was not sure what the final sum equalled. Now that I was no longer married to society, I was transitioning into something or someone else. What and who would that be? How could I describe this odd feeling of dissolving and recomposing? Words have to open the mind. When words close the mind, we can be sure that someone has been reduced to nothingness. **To amuse myself (there was no one else around) I began to think about the genre of the female nightdress in relation to plumbing.** The one I was wearing was black silk and I suppose quite sensual in a generic way. I could promenade in it and I could masquerade in it, given that femininity was a masquerade anyway. I could see that black silk was a classic in the female nightwear genre. To add to the mix, I was also wearing what my daughters called my 'shaman slippers'. They were black suede ankle boots trimmed with abundant, queasily realistic fake furs, one of which hung like a small tail, whipping my ankles as I walked around the flat looking for a gadget called a Master Plunger. The slippers were a gift from my best male friend, who thought I needed some 'insulation', as he put it — which might be a plumbing term for covering up something that is exposed and raw. I appreciated the fur boots with their comforting warmth and magical properties (I suppose my fantasy was that I had skinned the animals myself) and the postman's jacket seemed to be a counterpoint to the black silk nightdress. **I was the man. I was the woman.**

RATIONAL DRESS SOCIETY
on the Perfect Dress

Founded in London in 1881 by Lady Harberton, Mary Eliza Haweis and Constance Wilde, wife of Oscar, the Rational Dress Society set out to change the way women dressed and, in doing so, grant women a freedom in movement and society. The following are extracts from their manifesto and the catalogue of their inaugural exhibition of 1883.

THE RATIONAL DRESS SOCIETY PROTESTS against the introduction of any fashion in dress that either deforms the figure, impedes the movement of the body, or in any way tends to injure the health. It protests against the wearing of tightly-fitting corsets; of high-heeled shoes; of heavily-weighted skirts, as rendering healthy exercise almost impossible; and all tie down cloaks or other garments impeding on the movements of the arms. It protests against crinolines or crinolettes of any kind as ugly and deforming . . . [It] requires all to be dressed healthily, comfortably and beautifully, to seek what conduces to birth, comfort and beauty in our dress as a duty to ourselves and each other.

For Dress Reform it is necessary to gain the ear of two parties. If one only is gained, the Reform comes to a standstill. That is to say, we must gain not only those who wear dresses but those who make them; not only must the *demand* be created, but the *supply* be produced . . . The five requirements laid down in our circular would, if it were possible to carry them out completely, give a perfect dress – perfect in healthiness, comfort and beauty. But perfection is not possible of attainment in dress, any more

21

than in any other human work. We can only in this, as in every other undertaking, set our standard or principles as high as we can and then strive to meet them.

The attributes of the perfect dress:

1. Freedom of Movement
2. Absence of pressure over any part of the body
3. Not more weight than is necessary for warmth, and both weight and warmth evenly distributed
4. Grace and beauty combined with comfort and convenience
5. Not departing too conspicuously from the ordinary dress of the time

SIENNA MILLER
on Being Comfortable

Sienna is an award-winning actress and has been a style icon for more than twenty years. Her name became synonymous with Boho chic, the zeitgeist style of the Noughties, and in the process made her an expert on the challenges of style updates and the importance of knowing who you really are.

I'M NOT SURE I FULLY understood the power of fashion when I was younger. I chose clothes and accessories intuitively, just hoping I would look good. It hadn't really occurred to me that people would find particular meaning in those choices or want to construct a story about me from them. But of course, what we wear is powerful because it fundamentally shapes the way people perceive us. I was twenty-three when I started being photographed by the press and was just having fun with what I wore, being a little flamboyant and experimental with clothes as many of us are in our twenties. I wasn't prepared for the amount, or the tone, of the attention I received.

The Boho look I was tagged with was in the air back then. I didn't create it, I just wore it and got photographed in it. It was very 'me' at the time but, as the scrutiny grew, I started feeling self-conscious about it, and myself. I decided to pare back my style so that I attracted less attention. I eventually switched to a uniform of nice jeans and a good jumper because that allowed me to feel more comfortable and more authentic but was still chic. As I grew up, my lifestyle changed. Once I was a parent I didn't have time to trawl the markets looking for interesting pieces. I also became even less comfortable being looked at, though I think that's partly a function of age and stage of life. I'm hoping that by the time I'm sixty I will have gone back to being a flamboyant-dressing version of myself. I can feel it coming already. You just start to not give a shit!

For now, I'm really into elegance and beautiful tailoring so I buy Phoebe Philo-era Celine when I can find it on Vestiaire Collective. I like clothes that fit in an unusual way, and weird colours. At the moment I seem to be wearing lots of brown. I have a thing for shoes, especially boots, but I don't really care about handbags. Belts on the other hand . . . I love them. I love anything you can add to your classic uniform to give it a little lift. So my style is mostly about elegance and simplicity, though sometimes of course I just want to have fun and break out the sequins. What I wear is very mood dependent. If I'm staying with friends for a weekend then by the end of it I'll be wearing eight million scarves and a hat and loads of jewellery and having a lovely time. Boho is all still in there!

Being an actress, my style choices have definitely had an impact on the kind of work I've been offered. People in the business see you a certain way and that shapes the roles you are considered for. I don't think it's only actors or other people in the public eye who are affected by this, though. Style is social. It sends out signals. All of us are making judgements about others on the basis of what they're wearing, all the time. Sometimes those judgements are trivial but sometimes they're consequential.

So then there are decisions to be made: how much do I, or does anyone, want to use the power play of style choices in order to change our image and change the way people treat us? Using it in a deliberate way can be empowering but something is lost, I think, if it gets too calculated. In my line of work there's now a circular relationship between designers and actors when it comes to red carpet dressing, for example. Designers create outfits with that single moment in mind, which can end up having a restrictive effect on creativity.

Style and Substance

The reason I love the fashion and style of the 1960s and 1970s is that it sums up a much less self-conscious age. There's Jane Birkin with her perfect shirt and the best jeans and a little basket, or Brigitte Bardot, or anyone in the Rolling Stones. It's the freedom of the times reflected in the clothes that I find so inspiring. The mood was all wrapped up in music and design, and entwined with the revolution in sexual freedom and women's and civil rights. The way that people wore clothes back then feels so fresh. These days everything feels contrived.

We are living through an interesting moment in which, thanks to social media, we're all used to being looked at and have come to expect or even need it. Everyone's second guessing how we will appear to others. That inevitably has an effect on how we present ourselves. It can go in a number of different directions, of course. Clearly for many people it's liberating and empowering but I'm not sure it's a wholly positive thing. It feels harder to be spontaneous and genuinely free in our style choices. Everything is permitted but everything's also being done for the gaze of the audience. It's easy to lose yourself in that place. I'm not on social media at all because I'm just not comfortable with that level of self-exposure or scrutiny. Many of my friends are brilliant on those platforms and do it really well, but I know I wouldn't.

When you have a child your priorities change. There is now something and somebody who is infinitely more important than anything else. In the early years you have to give up a bit of yourself because the demands of the job are so big. I've found that the shift in mindset remains. My focus now is less 'how do I want to express myself?' and more 'how do I enable this person to express herself?' It's very grounding.

I've tried to raise my daughter to be confident in every aspect of life. It's necessary to be considerate of others, of course, but equally necessary not to lose sight of who she is, what she thinks, feels and needs. Times have changed since I was a child when the emphasis (especially for girls) was on being nice and polite at all costs. Any success I've had in this confidence-building is down to her, incidentally, not me. And she definitely has a sense of her own style. I've already discovered there's not much I can do to influence it.

I still love clothes but mostly I just want to look nice and be comfortable, though it's wonderful to be in a position to wear a beautiful dress from time to time. I've always wanted to feel like myself. I've never been very good at creating a persona to hide behind. I can totally see the appeal of that; it's just not very me. So I continue to try to dress in ways that feel instinctive and comfortable and then not worry too much about what I look like and who's watching.

The first piece I bought with my own money:

It was a white shearling-lined seventies coat that I bought from the vintage store What Goes Around Comes Around. It had an embroidered panel and the feel was a little bit Penny Lane. I bought the coat and a guitar with my first proper pay cheque. They were very expensive for me at the time. I don't know what happened to the coat but I still have the guitar.

Style and Substance

MEGAN JAYNE CRABBE
on Making Her Own Rules

Megan started posting about body positivity on Instagram back in 2016. She now has more than 1.2 million followers and is the author of the book *Body Positive Power*. When she wore a shimmering green gown with armpit hair dyed pink to match her mermaid tresses on the red carpet she proved, beyond a shadow of a doubt, that you can be size sixteen and super-stylish.

When I was very young, I loved clothes. My earliest memories of styling myself are full of bold prints and bright clashing colours. Most of my clothes were hand-me-downs that arrived every so often in a black bin bag from an older girl in the neighbourhood. I have a vivid memory of pulling out a pair of lime-green floral jeans that I would have worn every day if I could. I was conscious of the size label on clothes and which size I thought I 'should' be wearing, but it didn't stop me experimenting with colour or style – those anxieties manifested later on, when clothes became less about expression and more about disguise.

By the time I started struggling with my eating disorder, I was already firmly into my emo phase: everything was black, metal studs, layers of belts and pops of neon colour on chequered wristbands. Those clothes became a reflection of the angst I was feeling and also an attempt to find a community. I didn't grow up with much connection to different parts of my identity or culture and always felt 'different' in some way to people around me. Committing to the emo/goth/grunge aesthetic aligned me with others who also felt 'different'. Of course, as I got sicker, head-to-toe black was a convenient way of hiding myself.

27

After recovery, I started to reclaim colour – I felt alive again and wanted the way I dressed to reflect that. But it wasn't long before I found myself embedded back in diet culture and constantly chasing beauty standards as a way of finding happiness. During this period, the only determining factor for whether something was worth wearing was whether it was 'flattering' (i.e. did it made me look thinner?). There were a lot of draped fabrics, push-up bras, muted tones. Getting dressed wasn't joyful; it was a challenge based on moulding my body into something that would be worthy of being seen.

When I arrived in the world of body positivity, I banished the word 'flattering' from my wardrobe. I was determined to let myself wear all the things I'd told myself I wasn't allowed to, until I'd lost *x* pounds. I threw out my Spanx and bought bodycon dresses. I stopped wearing cardigans to cover up my arms, and embraced all the pastel hues that made me feel happy. The child-like whimsy of my style then was definitely amplified by being online and factoring in the reaction of an audience to the things I wore. I enjoyed always overdressing and being known for that bubblegum style.

These days, I think that has tempered slightly. I still love colour and embracing styles that some people claim aren't 'flattering' on a size sixteen body. But I prefer a bold tailored suit and heels to a fluffy unicorn-coloured dress. I wear what makes me feel powerful when I step onto a stage or get in front of a camera.

I love putting together red carpet looks – when I was around six years old I spent hours drawing clothes and cutting them out, mixing and matching different outfits together. When I'm deciding what to wear to a major event, it's kind of like that. I start with an idea – a theme, or one standout piece – and then I build around it, sketching out possibilities before going on the hunt for the missing elements. It is really satisfying when an outfit comes to life, especially knowing that you pulled it together with second-hand, borrowed, rented or small-business pieces.

I used to be absolutely hooked on fast fashion — a 'check out my haul!' kind of girl. Learning about the impact of fast fashion on the planet and the people who make our clothes turned me completely off that way of shopping and, for a few years now, I've only bought pre-loved clothes. I recently picked up a beautiful pink sequin minidress that I spotted an influencer wearing new about a year ago. I bided my time, searching regularly until I found one being sold on Vinted — it's extra satisfying when you finally find something you've wanted for a while!

I definitely have a conflicted relationship with style, given my values. On the one hand, I love adornment and creativity and colour. On the other hand, I hate how much we (especially women) have been taught to hyper-focus on appearance and base our worth on aesthetics alone. I worry about investing too much energy in the way I present myself, but the reality is that I work in an industry where appearance is relevant: how visually engaging your social media is determines how well your content performs; whether you look the part determines which events you're invited to. I have to be sure to balance out the days that are very appearance-focused with plenty of time embracing my natural state (which is usually bare-faced, no bra and joggers!) and working on things that aren't about aesthetics.

I'm constantly questioning why we feel the way we do about our bodies and how we present them. So much of what we take as fact is learned from misogynistic beauty standards — the idea that women shouldn't have body hair, or wear swimwear unless they have a flat stomach to go with it, for example. Rejecting those lessons sends a message to the younger version of me who was so obsessed with reaching the beauty standard that it was all she ever thought about: **we do not need to follow those rules to be worthy of the space we take up. We can make our own rules, using what feels right and leaving what doesn't.** And we're allowed to experiment. Self-expression should be fun, not punishing or obsessive.

The first piece I bought with my own money:

A pair of denim patchwork platform boots from Shoe Zone when I was about seven. My mum refused to buy them for me on the basis that I wouldn't get enough wear out of them, so I saved up my pocket money, went back, and proceeded to wear them every day to the most inappropriate of places, just to prove her wrong.

The one piece I'd save if my home was on fire:

A vintage Guess denim jacket with patches of pink, yellow and blue stripes. It's so rare to find true vintage in an XL; it felt like I'd found gold dust! It's so versatile, I wear it with all kinds of outfits and I've never seen anyone else with one, so I'd have to save her!

PAM GRIER
on Fitting Rooms

Dubbed the 'Queen of Blaxploitation', Pam Grier is a trail-blazing, stereotype-breaking actress who rose to fame for her starring roles in a number of 1970s action films including *Coffy* and *Foxy Brown*. Her various accolades include nominations for an Emmy Award, a Golden Globe Award, a Screen Actors Guild Award, a Satellite Award and a Saturn Award. The extract below is taken from her 2010 autobiography, *Foxy: My Life in Three Acts*.

I'D BEEN IN LOS ANGELES only a few weeks when I stood outside Judy's, an upscale women's West Los Angeles clothing store in Century City – the most beautiful store in the world, as far as I was concerned. I'd just been hired as a receptionist at a highly respected theatrical agency called the Agency for the Performing Arts (APA) on Sunset Boulevard, and I needed some appropriate work clothing. I gazed at the luxurious window designs featuring the hippest styles as I took a deep breath and got ready to walk inside. My hands were shaking. I suddenly wished my British co-worker from the office had come with me. She'd offered, but I'd declined, deciding to do this one alone. I wanted to spare her and myself the ultimate embarrassment and humiliation.

Shopping for work clothes should have been business as usual, and it probably would have been – if I didn't have dark skin and hadn't grown up when I did. Back then, in the early sixties, blacks were *not* allowed to try on clothing in any store in Denver or a lot of other U.S. cities. **We could go through the racks and choose what we liked, but we were barred from entering the**

dressing rooms. We had to buy the outfit (that eliminated choosing from several different things, because we didn't have enough money), take it home, and try it on. Apparently it was ok to try on the clothes, as long as the general public didn't have to witness it. Then we could keep it or return it — if it was still in the original bag with the receipt. No exceptions. If we lost a receipt or the bag, we didn't bother trying.

It was the same thing with shoes. What did we think — that we could put our common black feet into brand-new shoes in front of a white woman who might eventually purchase them? We had to buy the shoes, too, and try *them* on at home, out of view. Imagine the humiliation we went through just to go shopping. But then, hundreds of years ago, before the Civil War, an early Congress had deemed a black person three-fifths of a human being. These perceptions and labeling leave their scars, so I couldn't believe I was standing outside of Judy's, about to buy clothes like a regular adult.

I was accustomed to wearing jeans and Krista's hand-me-downs, which mostly consisted of wool sweaters, heels, and Timberland hiking boots for temperatures that would freeze your butt off. These boots were functional back then, not the fashion craze that they are today. The irony is that I was ahead of my time, wearing Timberlands that cost $9.95 at Sears instead of $175 at Nordstrom. But no one wore wool or heavy boots in balmy Southern California. I needed something new and different. Since the secretaries at APA didn't bat an eyelash when they heard that I was heading over to Judy's, maybe it was true — they really *did* let anyone try on clothes here.

I exhaled, pushed the door open, and stepped inside the store. I remained skeptical, even when a young white saleswoman walked towards me with a big smile. 'Can I help you?' she said pleasantly.

'Well,' I almost whispered, 'I'm looking for a white blouse and a black skirt. Something simple, comfortable, not expensive, that I can wash by hand and iron. They're for work.'

The saleswoman continued smiling as she took a moment to look me up and down, not to judge me but rather to assess my size. Then she began gathering several blouses and skirts for me to try, casually chatting all the while. 'The fitting rooms are right over there,' she said, pointing behind the checkout counter. 'Oh, here's something you might like.' She pulled a few more outfits from the rack, walked towards the fitting rooms, and hung the clothes on the hooks inside, expecting me to follow her.

'Really?' I said, standing where I was. 'Are you sure?'

She looked confused as I stood there, hesitating. 'Just go ahead,' she said, 'and let me know how they fit.'

I tried to look nonchalant, covering my amazement as best I could. When I stepped inside the fitting room and the saleswoman pulled the curtain closed, I had to catch my breath. My mother would never believe it, and neither would my friends back home. This is what we'd been protesting and marching for – to be treated like anyone else – and it was actually happening. I stood in the fitting room, holding back tears. **This was how it *should* be in the world,** the way my mum had envisioned it, and I couldn't wait to tell her.

CHLOË SEVIGNY
on Traditional-With-a-Twist

Chloë is an Academy Award-nominated actress, a director and a much-admired fashion and style maverick and trendsetter. She was scouted on the streets of New York at the age of sixteen, and at the age of nineteen she starred in *Kids*, the era-defining movie of the 1990s. She hasn't stopped since.

I'VE ALWAYS LOVED PLAYING WITH clothes. As a child I lived in my own fantasy world, making up games and acting out little plays. My parents encouraged it. My mom was a thrifter way before anybody thought it was cool, and she would pick out bits and pieces for my dress-up box when she went shopping. It was full of hats and shawls, sequined dresses, feathered boas, prairie dresses and cowgirl boots. One summer I wore a Wonder Woman bathing suit twenty-four hours a day, every day. Even when I was tiny, I wanted to be expressive through clothing. I just never grew out of my desire to play dress-up.

My mother was a born recycler and frugal woman who loved a bargain. The thrifts in town were gold mines, full of Laura Ashley dresses or polo shirts I might be coveting. So my mom took me to the thrift stores, to hunt until we found what we wanted. It was really unusual back then to buy second-hand; it was almost weird, but it was just what we did. My mom normalised it for me. She instilled in me the thrill of the hunt.

Both she and my dad enjoyed clothes themselves. They appreciated quality and thoughtful design and sheer beauty. I remember a specific birthday or Christmas when my dad bought my mother an Hermès scarf. I remember the beautiful orange box arriving

— the packaging was impossibly glamorous, the designs were exqui-site. For my eighteenth birthday my parents went halfsies with me to buy a pair of Margiela Tabis from IF in Soho. I had been obsessed with them for a year, but they were wildly expensive for a teenager. I still wear them.

I was lucky to have parents who supported my interest in dance and theatre and fashion, who related to it themselves. As a teen-ager I was desperate to leave our small town in Connecticut and get into New York City. I would beg my dad to take me into NYC so I could hang out at the Fiorucci store, hoping to catch a glimpse of Madonna or Cyndi Lauper because I'd read some-where that they shopped there. He would indulge me for an hour or so and then say, ever so gently, 'Maybe they're not coming today, Chloë,' and take me to Saks to soothe me with a little window shopping. My family took a lot of pleasure in style and expressed a lot of love through clothes and fashion.

All of these elements came together when I was trying to choose what to wear on my wedding day. I'd never really thought very much about wedding dresses beyond assuming that if I ever married, I would wear one of my favourite vintage gowns – some-thing I'd had for years. However, when the moment came, I was just overwhelmed by the pressure of what to wear for such a big moment in my life. I'm lucky to have worked with a stylist, Haley Wollens, for many years, who was very helpful and constructive during this daunting wedding dress process. In the end I had three outfits; one for the ceremony, one for the dinner and one I could dance in, at the party. I got married in my hometown, in a local church, with all my family and friends around me, and then after the reception, we went to a party at my brother's bar back in the City. The dress I wore for the church ceremony was full-length and white and very deconstructed, almost tattered, with a high neck, long sleeves and a train designed by Glenn Martens for Gaultier Couture. A little bit traditional and a little bit alternative. I felt like a sea anemone or a siren washed up on the shore in that dress. It was a magical moment of dressing up, a fantasy like the childhood games I'd played with the same friends who were there that day. I think that's what people want to feel at a wedding: both rooted in their community and also transported into a fantasy of love. That was what I hoped to project and that was how I felt in all three of my dresses.

Even as a teenager, I loved that traditional-with-a-twist aesthetic. The ability to make something classic feel different appealed to me. It was why I loved Dave Gahan from Depeche Mode, who would wear a black turtleneck and jeans and black loafers and make it look like such a special version of something everyday. I was always striving for that.

There was also a large dose of the usual teenage desire to be different and to show the world that I was not just a blonde, blue-eyed Connecticut girl. I was obsessed with New Wave, grunge and punk and being alternative. That was so important to me when I was in high school. I wanted to project all my passions through my clothing, and really let that freak flag fly.

A lot of my inspiration came from the British style magazines like *i-D*, *The Face* and *Dazed* who were talking about those alternative scenes and elevating fashion in such an interesting, cool way. They covered Seattle grunge and minimalist avant-garde fashion far more closely than the US magazines. They were a touchstone for me; I just devoured them. A lot of my style as a kid was born out of insecurity. I thought I needed *more* in order to be interesting. I'm not even sure about more of what. More layers or accessories, perhaps, or more jewellery, more make-up. Seeing how photographers like Corinne Day were shooting fashion taught me that you really don't need much. You can have one cool piece, and simply by being yourself, you can create a look.

I spent years wanting to be part of the scene I was reading about and could see around me in the city. And then, from one day to another, I was. I got scouted for *i-D* on the street in New York and suddenly I was in the pages of the magazine I loved, wearing a Comme des Garçons dress. My life took a different turn. I can see that playing out in my high school graduation photo. I was seventeen, wearing something I'd cobbled together from thrift stores under my cap and gown, and around my neck is a pendant I made myself from lace ribbon with a piece of boxwood tied to it. I'd seen something like it on the Margiela catwalk that year and wanted to copy it. It summed up everything I wanted to be as I left high school behind. The punk ethos of using found pieces, the simple shape of the wood and the contrast with the lace, the minimalist elegance.

I've always tried to figure out what it is I want to project with my clothes and aim for that, rather than concern myself with the labels other people use. I've been called an 'It girl' and my style has been described as both 'cool' and 'elegant'. Obviously these are flattering terms and I'd rather be applauded for my style than not, but I think any moniker is pretty hard to swallow and even harder to maintain. I'm now the forty-eight-year-old mother of a three-year-old son. When I'm hanging out in the playground I'm not thinking about being cool or elegant!

I'm trying to figure out what style means to me at this stage in my life. I just did a big closet clean out and sold quite a lot of clothes to raise money for charity and for the cost of storing those pieces I do want to keep. It was an interesting process. I had to ask myself a lot of questions. Do I still want to wear a Peter Pan collar? Am I really going to keep this dress I can't fit into any more? Or all these jeans? Will my son want them one day? I know I would have loved a stack of vintage jeans when I was a teen, but will he?

Since I had my son I'm not the shape I used to be. I've got boobs now. I'm curvier. It's taken me a long time to get used to that and I still struggle. Our minds are very powerful when it comes to telling us how to feel about our bodies. It's crazy how powerful that shame can be, though it also makes sense given that we still see only a very restricted range of bodies in the media.

It's hard to navigate midlife style but I'm finding it helpful to ask, as I always have done, what it is I want to project about myself and my life. I no longer need to be seen as alternative or cool. Maybe I'm transitioning into a more graceful phase. Effortless grace: that seems very desirable to me now I'm nearing fifty with a young child. Maybe I'll start wearing knee-length skirts, Yohji Yamamoto, 1980s Comme des Garçons, channelling the gallerist Mary Boone and Carolyn Bessette-Kennedy.

This is the thing about clothes: they help define us. They are like a weapon, or at least a tool. There's great joy to be found in defining ourselves through style but it's never completely immune to the power of other people's expectations and judgements. That's why I try to focus on *my* pleasure, *my* desire. What do I want my clothes to say? I love the freedom to move around between style moods. To use a modern word, I like the fluidity of navigating between all of them.

Style icons and influences:

Hollywood Golden-era film stars, especially Marlene Dietrich, in her menswear inspired garb.
The 1940s in general, especially as seen by the 1970s. Yves Saint Laurent's take on that period is one of my ultimate style touchstones. Women like Bianca Jagger and Debbie Harry, Cookie Mueller, Grace Jones, who embody that 'rolled in the street' 1970s New York glamour. They ooze sex appeal and intelligence and streetwise confidence.
Rainer Werner Fassbinder's movies.
Japanese street fashion from the 1990s.
Jean Paul Gaultier, especially when he dressed Madonna during her Blond Ambition period.

Style and Substance

38

The first piece I bought with my own money:

I was fourteen, going on fifteen, and determined to set a new tone for eighth grade. I planned the outfit I would wear on the first day back meticulously, and put it together from pieces I'd bought over the summer vacation. I went into school wearing a navy-blue, cropped turtleneck sweater with a miniskirt, striped stockings and wing-tipped DMs. I thought I was the coolest girl in the world. I was like, 'This is who I am now . . .'

The one piece I'd save if my home was on fire:

Most of the clothes I want to keep are in storage, so I'm not certain there's anything else I'd dive back in to rescue. Perhaps the dress I wore to the Oscars when I was nominated for *Boys Don't Cry* – if that were in the house, I'd go back for it. It's a simple black halterneck gown, Yves Saint Laurent by Alber Elbaz. I wore his clothes when I was doing press for the film and I found them comforting and empowering. I don't particularly love being on the red carpet – I don't always feel like myself by the time I've had hair and make-up done. But on that night, I felt wonderful. I wanted a classic film-star look that wouldn't date, so I wore the black dress with a heavy platinum and diamond necklace, red nails and lipstick and my short hair in a forties-style, set in curls. Alber helped me achieve my dream of old Hollywood glamour.

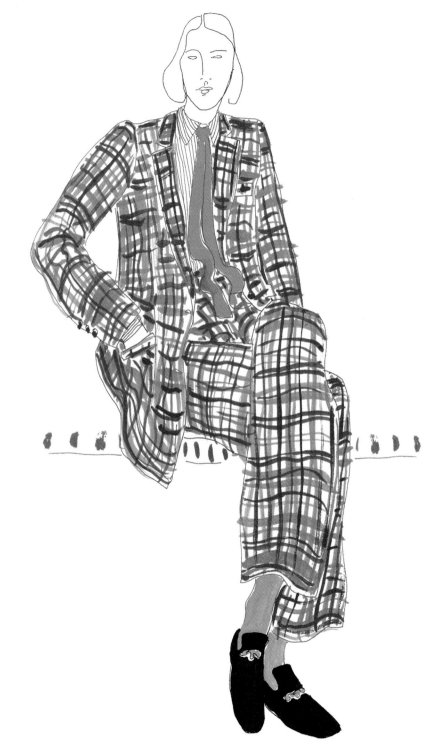

PART 2

RULES

'One should always dress like a marble column.'

JACKIE KENNEDY

BELLA FREUD
on the Charm of a Suit

Bella is a designer of fashion and interiors, a filmmaker and artist whose works combine irreverence and lightly worn intellectual curiosity about the world. Her iconic knitwear and immaculate tailoring have gained her cult status.

A CONSIDERED, STYLISH CHOICE OF clothing can transform how you feel. When I was about ten I was into boyish clothes. My mother didn't have much money so we used to go to jumble sales and I would look for boys' shirts, enormous on me, and cut the ends off the sleeves to fit. There was something about them that I loved. Then, one day, I suddenly understood what it was. I remember looking in the mirror and feeling unhappy. Then I changed into one of those cut-down shirts and immediately I saw myself differently, so I felt different: confident and at ease. It was a eureka moment for me, the realisation that I could change how I felt about myself by playing with the relationship between my clothes, my reflection and my emotions.

When I got older I started to look for more feminine styles but I still loved things that had morphed out of clothes for boys. My cut-down shirts turned into shirt dresses. My clothing couldn't ever be haphazard; it had to serve a purpose, and the purpose was to enhance my feelings. I would wear certain things again and again: black flares, a black T-shirt with mirrored sequins. I'm still a bit like that, actually. There is something very luxurious about returning over and over to a piece or a style that you love and that makes you confident. Today I'm wearing one

43

of my black-and-white 1970 sweaters, for example, which I wear on repeat. (I do have five of them, admittedly.)

I like to make things that people can wear for ever, though of course it's also important to have new clothes from time to time because you need to reinvent yourself slightly in order to stay interesting to yourself. I love to feel comfortable but I don't ever want to feel cosy, which risks being too familiar. I want to feel good, agile, deft — and so much of that is to do with having the right outfit. **I want to feel like a ninja who has the perfect suit. You can sleep in it, fight in it, go to dinner in it, seduce in it.** But it has to be immaculate.

At the moment I'm going through a phase of, 'If in doubt, dress up rather than down.' Most of my life it's been the other way around. I've never wanted to seem like an attention seeker. Now I think, 'Too bad. Time is short. I'm going to wear my best suit.' Perhaps I'm outgrowing an inner critic.

Being stylish is undoubtedly more to do with what you think of yourself than what others think of you, but it can be hard not to care about people's opinions. When I was a child I was very aware that dressing differently would draw attention, and that the quality of that attention depended on questions of power and privilege. My mother was very beautiful and she was a hippy at a time and in a place where people really didn't like hippies. How she dressed reflected who she was, but being poor and unconventional attracted negative attention and made her vulnerable.

My father, on the other hand, was also somebody who dressed in ways that marked him out from other people but he had power, prestige and money, which allowed him to be independent of others' thoughts and comments. He often looked glamorous, though sometimes he looked like a tramp: clothes full of holes. When he wore Savile Row suits and grey flannel it was always with a scarf rather than a tie. He never tried to blend in. He pleased himself. There is a tightrope that leads the stylish dresser towards either attack or admiration, and my parents went their own ways.

Attack can evolve into admiration, of course. One of my first jobs in fashion was with Vivienne Westwood, who was admired at first by a very particular group of people and denounced by everyone else. Later she was universally admired, without ever changing her style. She was a great influence on me, though we were not similar. She was an inventor of fashion; I am not that. But I saw how hard she worked. How much she had to persevere in order to get anywhere. I had seen it in my father, too. I think every act of creativity — including the creation of a style — requires you to work through your frustration when something isn't going well. It isn't about inspiration; it's about application. Though a little inspiration is helpful to get you started.

I look to art and literature and music for ideas about what to design and what to wear. I'm voracious about it. Perhaps that's because I didn't have a proper education. I left school at sixteen, but I have always read everything I could get my hands on. I discovered that I visualise the characters I'm reading about, very strongly. Sometimes the visualisation I conjure up when I'm reading is almost stronger than the image I see when I look at a film or a painting.

When I was in my twenties and starting out as a designer, I came across the novels by the French writer Colette, about her character Claudine. I was captivated by this girl. She was so naughty and so fierce. I thought, 'I want to dress Claudine.' So I did. It was clear to me what she would have worn if she were around in the 1990s when I started to design. She'd be wearing Coco Chanel but micro-miniskirts; knitted soft fabrics that clung but also covered up. The sort of clothes that a girl would wear to announce she was subverting the codes of her bourgeois background. Designing for Claudine allowed me to distil as much meaning as possible into clothes that were not overt, shocking or loud. I've been refining that process ever since, more recently with my tailoring and with my slogan knitwear and T-shirts.

Perhaps it's my father's influence, or my own early taste for

45

boys' clothes, but I have always been fascinated by the possibilities of a suit. Ever since I was a child I have wanted to take that safe unit and tweak it. I used to envy boys their school uniform, which though it was imposed on them could be endlessly tinkered with, to signal their identity. Suiting is so minimal, which means that even a tiny adjustment can be dramatic. And the charm of a suit . . . A good suit frames the face, enhances a person's look of thoughtfulness and intelligence. **As a teenager I became obsessed with the elegance of bus conductors' uniforms,** the way they gave dignity to the people doing the job. Later, when I lived in Rome, I studied tailoring. I learned about the interior work that goes on inside a jacket, the decorative work involved in a button-hole. I observed that some people wanted others to know about the suit they were wearing. If they turned the cuffs back to show off the craftsmanship, for example, that might signal the difference between an aristocrat who'd been wealthy for generations and a spivvy mafioso. The way we wear clothes, the gestures we create with them — all that is the essence of personal style.

This drive to distil meaning into clothes led me to using words and phrases as decoration on knitwear. Language is crucial to me. I love to look at the banners that people make for protests: what are the personal slogans they want to carry with them? There's something so moving about the words that people choose to put on themselves. Pedantic messaging is rarely effective but language can send an oblique signal that communicates because it's intriguing. I also love the patterns that words create. Sometimes I find a word is perfect for a sock but would be too weighty for a sweater. In one place it might be provocative, in another it takes on a sweeter tone.

Style is our clothes' capacity to speak for us in disarming or intriguing ways. When we get our clothes right, it shows people another aspect of ourselves that they wouldn't necessarily have apprehended. An actress friend of mine wore one of my suits to do an interview with the press and she showed this cool and shy side of herself that you only discover when you get to know her. I love the way we can collaborate with our clothes to communicate more, and differently.

This is what's so magical about style, and it's deeply powerful. I have felt that power myself, many times. When I was a girl obsessed with Colette's Claudine, I channelled Coco Chanel as she emerged from her convent school and began to make her way in the world. I had a favourite outfit, a velvet chiffon striped dress with a matching cardigan coat, which I wore with a crisp white shirt underneath so that the collar peeked out above the dress. It must have cost all of £2 second-hand but it was such a distinct look and it communicated what I was thinking about in a way that seemed to surprise people. That gave me a lot of confidence. I was tremendously shy but I felt I could let the outfit do some of the work. It bought me time to think, when someone spoke to me.

People respond to this powerful magic when they see it, and once you notice, you see it everywhere. Whether it's Tilda Swinton in the pale-blue suit I made for her or a child deciding very deliberately to wear *this* skirt with *those* tights or clash it with *that* sweater, a stylish choice is one that draws attention to a person's way of thinking and being. I still find it mesmerising. Caring about what you wear is sometimes regarded as vain or superficial but I see it as a tool, a practicality. In rain, you need Wellingtons. In life, you will have to navigate events, emotions and people. If you're wearing a good outfit, it's easier. **The right clothes just make everything better.**

The first piece I bought with my own money:

When I was a schoolgirl, my friends and I used to visit the market in East Grinstead, the local town. There were a couple of Indian stallholders who imported beautiful things, the kind you'd imagine Carole King wearing . . . with pintucks like Victorian blouses but perfect for the seventies. We couldn't afford those fabrics so we bought the cheesecloth tops. I remember buying a pair of simple white trousers from one of the stalls. The fall of the fabric, the proportion . . . They silenced my inner critic. They were just perfect.

The one piece I'd save if my home was on fire:

It would have to be my 1970 jumper, with the gold stripe running from the black rollneck down each sleeve. Even if I had nothing else and had to wear a bin bag tied round my waist as a skirt, with this jumper I would feel fine. I would still be me.

COLETTE
on Being Blasé

Sidonie-Gabrielle Colette, known simply as Colette, was a French writer during the first half of the twentieth century. Her semi-autobiographical, unwittingly feminist and somewhat salacious Claudine series follows the growth to maturity of a rebellious and spirited heroine. This extract is from the first novel, *Claudine à l'école*.

AMONG THE SCHOOLGIRLS, IT WAS very much the thing not to seem in the least concerned about what one was going to wear for the prizegiving. All of them were brooding over it a month in advance and tormenting their Mamas to be allowed ribbons or lace or at least alterations which would bring last year's dress up to date – but **it was considered good taste to say nothing** about it. We asked each other with detached curiosity, as if out of politeness: 'What's your dress going to be like?' And we appeared hardly to listen to the answer, made in the same off-hand contemptuous tone.

The gawky Anaïs had asked me the routine question, her eyes elsewhere and her face vacant. With an absent-minded look, and sounding quite indifferent, I explained: 'Oh, nothing startling . . . white muslin . . . a crossed fichu on the bodice, with the neck cut down to a point . . . and Louis XV sleeves with a muslin frill, stopping at the elbows . . . That's all.'

LEO TOLSTOY
on Natural Artifice

Widely regarded as one of the greatest writers of all time, Tolstoy was nominated multiple times for both the Nobel Prize in Literature and the Nobel Peace Prize. He is best known for *War and Peace* and *Anna Karenina*, which was published in instalments between 1875 and 1877, and from which the following extract is taken.

ALTHOUGH HER DRESS, HER COIFFURE, and all the preparations for the ball had cost Kitty great trouble and consideration, at this moment she walked into the ballroom in her elaborate tulle dress over a pink slip as easily and simply as though all the rosettes and lace, all the minute details of her attire, had not cost her or her family a moment's attention, as though she had been born in that tulle and lace, with her hair done up high on her head, and a rose and two leaves on the top of it.

When, just before entering the ballroom, the princess, her mother, tried to turn right side out of the ribbon of her sash, Kitty had drawn back a little. She felt that everything must be right of itself, and graceful, and nothing could need setting straight.

It was one of Kitty's best days. Her dress was not uncomfortable anywhere; her lace berthe did not droop anywhere; her rosettes were not crushed nor torn off; her pink slippers with high, hollowed-out heels did not pinch, but gladdened her feet; and the thick rolls of fair chignon kept up on her head as if they were her own hair. All the three buttons buttoned up without tearing on the long glove that covered her hand without concealing its lines. The black velvet of her locket nestled with special softness round her neck. That velvet was delicious; at home, looking at her neck in the looking glass, Kitty had felt that that velvet was speaking. **About all the rest there might be a doubt, but the velvet was delicious.** Kitty smiled here too, at the ball, when she glanced at it in the glass. Her bare shoulders and arms gave Kitty a sense of chill marble, a feeling she particularly liked. Her eyes sparkled, and her rosy lips could not keep from smiling from the consciousness of her own attractiveness.

STANLEY TUCCI
on Dressing for the Occasion

Stanley Tucci is a former bartender, multi-award-winning actor and filmmaker, and star of the hit TV show *Stanley Tucci: Searching for Italy*. His memoir *Taste: My Life Through Food*, has been a bestseller all over the world. During the lockdowns triggered by the Covid pandemic, Stanley's online cocktail-making tutorials caused something of a stir.

TO TAKE STYLE SERIOUSLY IS a sign of respect for yourself, for those around you and for the artisans that created your clothes.

Personally, I like to dress very simply and in a way that is appropriate for the season and the occasion. My taste is what I would describe as 'classic'. I don't care for the way that a busy pattern looks on me, for example, but I do like narrow stripes and muted plaids.

I take inspiration from Italian style, from old Hollywood and from vintage menswear, in particular from the 1920s to the early 1960s. There are so many sartorial lessons to be learned from those eras. Then, from the late sixties onwards, everything started to change. Some of the clothes from that period are great, but polyester eventually altered the look and feel of everything, not necessarily for the better. Dressing up in everyday life became less and less important. These days, many people don't dress nicely to go out to dine or to the theatre, which I find sad. To dress for an occasion, no matter how small, is to shift out of the mundane. **Celebrating an event's importance with our clothes is one of the easiest ways to give shape, weight and significance to our lives.** This ability of clothes to define differences is part of their importance, but sadly there is now less diversity in the way people dress across the world. Global connectivity has brought cultures closer but created a sameness in the way we dress. You do still see the Savile Row-suited men in London and the elegant cuts worn by men in Florence, but less so all the time. There are too many sneakers, sweatpants and T-shirts sporting logos. I find them hateful.

Wearing costumes is part of my professional life and can be great fun besides helping you to find or create the character. When I was working on *The Devil Wears Prada*, for example, I learned a great deal from Patricia Field, the costume designer. She was unafraid to put what one might think would be clashing patterns and fabrics together. I think I spent more time in costume fittings than I did on set, but I didn't mind because they were so interesting and fun. Also, I suspect that most actors are delighted when their character has to wear a military uniform, especially one from the nineteenth or early twentieth century. Those uniforms are tailored just so and have huge presence. In my personal life, by contrast, I will do everything I can to wear only those clothes I have chosen and that make me feel comfortable. Costume could not be further from my mind.

Style, for me, has always been associated with taste and extends far beyond the clothes we wear. My parents were my teachers in this regard. As a small child I loved watching them dress for a night out. The ceremony of it, the specialness. They always looked so well put together. They also placed great importance on how a cocktail was made, a table was set, how dinner was cooked and served – on a daily basis, but especially for guests and on holidays. I am a product of their good taste. Which is not to say that I grew up with money. I did not. Taste has nothing to do with money and certainly cannot be bought, though I believe that good taste can help you find a way to make money if you choose.

Ultimately, what matters is that what you wear is right for you. I feel I've found my true style over the last decade. I don't imagine it will change much before I die.

QUENTIN BELL
on Fashion as Science

The son of Vanessa Bell, a member of the Bloomsbury group, Quentin Bell was an art historian and the official biographer of his aunt, Virginia Woolf. In 1947 he published *On Human Finery*, a meditation on our relationship with clothes.

THE STUDY OF FASHION . . . is a borderline science, important to the historian in that it exhibits in a pure form the changing impulse of social behaviour; to the artist in that here, if anywhere, we can trace a direct relationship between economics and aesthetics . . .

Who does not appreciate the expense, the inconvenience, perhaps even the discomfort of that which they feel themselves compelled to wear? In obeying fashion we undergo discomforts and distresses which are, from a strictly economic point of view, needless and futile. We do so for the sake of something which transcends our own immediate interests. What we may conveniently call our 'baser nature' protests against the tyranny of tailors and dressmakers, but we are continually urged upwards and on by a sense of what is decent, correct and comely, and though there are many who fail there are but few who will deliberately flout the categorical imperative of fashion.

Our clothes are too much part of ourselves for us ever to be entirely indifferent to their condition; the feeling of being perfectly dressed imparts a buoyant confidence to the wearer, and it impresses the beholder as though the fabric were indeed a natural extension of the man.

JAMES BALDWIN
on Elegant Despair

James Baldwin (1924–87) was an American writer and activist whose eloquence about race, sexuality and class made him an influential figure in the civil rights movement. In *No Name in the Street*, he poignantly recounts his Harlem childhood, the tragic assassinations of Martin Luther King Jr and Malcolm X, and his return to a tumultuous and divided America.

I COULD NOT PUT IT **on without a bleak, pale, cold wonder about the future.** I could not, in short, live with it: it was too heavy a garment. Yet — it was only a suit, worn, at most, three times. It was not a very expensive suit, but it was still more expensive than any my friend could buy. He could not afford to have suits in his closet which he didn't wear, he couldn't afford to throw suits away — he couldn't, in short, afford my elegant despair.

FRAN LEBOWITZ
on Caring

A sardonic, satirical writer and a quintessential New Yorker, in 1984 Fran Liebowitz told the *New York Times*, 'I hate to go shopping, I can't stand it.' In an interview with US *Elle*, she explained how she takes care of the jeans, jacket, shirt and boots that have long formed her signature look.

I ALWAYS WORE 501 LEVI'S. They used to make them in San Francisco. Every size was the same size, which sounds obvious, but you would be surprised — and then, I don't know, at some point during globalization they started making them in Mexico, and like every other thing they branched out to places you'd never heard of. So now every single size of Levi's is a different size. They cost less, too, which doesn't make any sense. I wish that real estate were cheaper and clothes were more expensive. But that's what young people want: $2 T-shirts that fall apart in the wash.

People care more about trends now than they do about style. They get so wrapped up in what's happening that they forget how to dress, and they never learn who they are because they never learn how to take care of anything. So much of what my generation was taught regarding clothes was how to make them last. How to wash and care for them.

I take very good care of my clothes. When I get home, I instantly hang up my jacket. If it's hot outside, I'll hang it on the shower rod so that it can air out a bit before I put it away. That's the first thing I do. Then I'll hang up my shirt if I'm going to wear it again that night, and I change into another shirt that I just wear around the house. It's from high school and has holes in it. I love it because it's mine and because nobody sees me in it, ever. I put my cufflinks in their little box. I shoeshine once a week. My jeans go in the washing machine, my shirts go out (they're starched), and my clothes that need to be dry-cleaned go to the most expensive dry-cleaner. I dry-clean as infrequently as possible — not only because it's psychotically expensive, but also because who knows what it does to the clothes? Dry . . . clean. These words don't go together. Wet clean — that is how you clean. I can't even imagine the things they do at the drycleaner. I don't want to know.

JOAN DIDION
on Packing

Joan Didion was a celebrated American writer known not only for her incisive essays and novels, but also for her effortlessly chic wardrobe. With her trademark sunglasses and minimalist style, she became an icon in the fashion world during the 1960s and 1970s. In 2015, at the age of eighty, she became the face of Céline. The packing list below is taken from her memoir, *The White Album*.

TO PACK AND WEAR:
2 skirts
2 jerseys or leotards
1 pullover sweater
2 pair shoes
stockings
bra
nightgown, robe, slippers
cigarettes
bourbon
bag with:
— shampoo
— toothbrush and paste
— Basis soap, razor
— deodorant
— aspirin
— prescriptions
— Tampax
— face cream
— powder
— baby oil

TO CARRY:
mohair throw
typewriter
2 legal pads and pens
files
house key

THIS IS A LIST WHICH was taped inside my closet door in Hollywood during those years when I was reporting more or less steadily. The list enabled me to pack, without thinking, for any piece I was likely to do. **Notice the deliberate anonymity of costume**: in a skirt, a leotard, and stockings, I could pass on either side of the culture. Notice the mohair throw for trunk-line flights (i.e. no blankets) and for the motel room in which the air conditioning could not be turned off. Notice the bourbon for the same motel room. Notice the typewriter for the airport, coming home: the idea was to turn in the Hertz car, check in, find an empty bench, and start typing the day's notes.

ZADIE SMITH
on London Versus New York Style

Zadie Smith gained international recognition with her
multi-award-winning debut novel *White Teeth*, which was
published in 2000 when she was just twenty-four years
old. Now, with many more books and countless prizes
under her (no doubt fashionable) belt, she continues
to write regularly for the *New Yorker* and the *New York
Review of Books* and is a tenured professor of Creative
Writing at New York University. This piece on transatlantic style was first published in British *Vogue*.

I WORK IN AN AMERICAN university, but in the long academic
holidays I come home, to England. Twice a year — and for the
past 10 years — I've stood before an open suitcase in New York
and thought: *what do people wear in London?* Or, conversely, if the
suitcase is in London: *what do they wear in New York?* I always forget,
I never get it right. I've turned up on a Tuesday night at a local
pub dressed as you might for a quick pre-dinner cocktail with a
girlfriend in Tribeca. (These are not the same outfits.) I've rocked
up to Hampstead Heath for a picnic looking about ready for the
Afropunk festival in Fort Greene. (Also not the same outfits.)
A decade of travelling back and forth can create sartorial schiz-
ophrenia — but you learn a lot, too. For example: it's perfectly
acceptable, in New York, to put all your tragic mid-life-crisis
energy into outdressing every other parent at Family Morning,
yet in London, this is considered bad form. (A performance of
maternal chaos is preferred.)

If you go on holiday with Londoners, you can take a 'capsule
wardrobe', if you like. No one will ridicule you as you model

your various outfits around a small Cornish town chock-a-block with screaming toddlers. (Of course, despite what the Sunday style sections may suggest, no one will pay you any mind, either.) But if you go on holiday with New Yorkers, any deviation from denim shorts, white shirt and the plainest possible sandals will make you look like a try-hard fool. You can't stand an hour in line for lobster rolls in a pair of platform espadrilles.

London women believe in a second layer: cardigan, hoodie, shacket. New York women, in my experience, do not. They'd rather a long-sleeve blouse, a cashmere sweater, or the kind of brightly coloured, expensive, delicate spring coat you can wear in New York for exactly nine days in May. In both cities, as far as I can tell, the heel as daywear is dead. Not as dead as it is in Paris, where you rarely see a young woman out of trainers – but still pretty dead. This past summer, I was having lunch with my friend Ashley when a woman hobbled by our window in *Sex and the City*-era 5in stilettos and the whole restaurant stopped eating, curious to see if she'd make it to the next corner. Poor lady: she'd not gotten the memo. Yet in a way I admired her, for **New York can be oppressive when it comes to memos.** Take me and Ashley: two lady writers having lunch, hadn't seen each other for a while, and yet – same outfit. A-line tent dress with massive arm flaps; flat sandals, huge earrings, huge glasses; no make-up except lipstick, wild Afros. Angela Davis goes to Palm Beach. Where do such memos come from? I get that the fashion-industrial complex usually has a hand in starting them, but these crazes also seem to have localised areas of intensity, which then spread. I first became aware of the boilersuit in the early noughties, as it radiated out of Brooklyn, penetrated an initially resistant Manhattan, and then crossed the Atlantic, with the consequence that I now spend about three months of the year wearing boilersuits, which feel to me as neutral a piece of clothing as a pair of Levi's once were. It's a long time since I wore Levi's. In both cities, Levi's are now for the young, worn mom-style, pulled up to the belly button and accompanied by a cropped white vest or a brutally ugly throwback sweater with a comedy logo (Care Bears, The Simpsons, DARE), or a clearly flammable shellsuit top, or a normcore flannel shirt, vintage crap, all of which looks inexplicably fabulous – on them. I think of it as a form of generation Z revenge dressing, intended to demonstrate – to the generation that crashed the economy and despoiled the planet – that we can't buy back our youth or return to 1991 to reclaim what's been lost. They wear it well.

Mass-market cheap clothes have a different life here and there. In New York, they tend to be poorly cut, with loose buttons and sticky zips. Often they look as if they've been constructed out of the remains of a ghost net, and rarely survive three washes. They do look good when brand new, but, again, mostly the young seem to benefit, or whoever can be bothered to trawl Lower Broadway on a weekly basis. In London, cheap clothes are so good, so plentiful, that only the very foolish and uncreative fail to make use of them. It's the delight of the Londoner to turn up to a wedding or a club looking a million dollars in an outfit that cost £49.99, thus demonstrating a good eye, canny style and admirable thriftiness. Nobody in London is impressed by the branded bags, shoes and watches that New York women always look so proud to own and yet whose only possible message to the passing observer is that there's money in them there hills. Cheap kids' clothes, in England, are of astonishing quality when compared with their American equivalent. Every September our children are flattered at the school gate by Americans who have no idea that when I say, 'It's a brand called George,' this means I bought it for a tenner in a supermarket called Asda.

'Unending beauty, ever fresh, ever new, very cheap and within the reach of everybody, bubbles up every day of the week from an inexhaustible well.' That's Virginia Woolf writing about the experience of shopping on Oxford Street. The only update required is our present guilty awareness of the ugly labour conditions underpinning our fast-fashion pleasures. Most Londoners don't brave Oxford Street very often, but they go to the identical stores in their own hoods, and pick through the piles for a bargain. If you're clever about it, as my mother is, these purchases act as a base against which to set off your own more fabulous items, in her case, a collection of South African Zulu crowns, that look even more regal combined with a shiny minidress rescued from the sale rack at the back of Cricklewood's Matalan. The first ennobles the second, until you can't tell the difference. **I was born into this London habit of mix and match and I cannot change it in New York.** My 'Rachel Comey' white heels are actually Zara, all my 'gold' and 'silver' hoop earrings are from branches of the Duane Reade pharmacy, and my fanciest under-wear can be bought in packs of 10 at Gap. However, New York has instilled in me the importance of tailoring, of a good dress that reaches to the knee and can be worn anywhere, and of the kind of well-made brogues in which you can walk 40 blocks – and I spend too much money on all of them. I look around and see that I am not alone. Notwithstanding the aforementioned cult of youth, grown-up dressing is respected and celebrated in New York, and constantly supported by other grown-up women who will stop you in the street, sometimes several times a day, if they see something they admire. I don't think there's a higher compliment in this world than being stopped by a stylish 50-year-old and asked where you got your winter coat. (It is, in terms of its effect on the spirit, the exact opposite of being cat-called by a bloke in a van.)

In the New York summer, things get more complicated: few can remain stylish in that heat. The temptation to go floaty and diaph-anous is strong, like a net curtain awaiting a passing breeze. I hate floaty. And diaphanous. Thankfully there is very little boho spirit in Manhattan, and hardly anyone spends the season in those long, flowy, tasselled or fringed garments that you do seem to get a lot of in London, and which entail being able to create a silhouette out of the natural contrast between your waist and the rest of your body. Having no waist, I can't rely on such fripperies. And though crisp, tailored shorts or the kind of summer dresses that need ironing will get you some strange looks in the London parks (where wrinkled linen and cotton sundresses abide), in New York, summer proves no obstacle to a certain formality. Formality. Is that the key difference? Brooklyn would laugh at the suggestion, but to my eye both Brooklyn's transplanted hipsters and its original natives appear — when compared with their London equivalents in Shoreditch or Harlesden — somehow more arch, more obviously stylised, more in costume, more like someone on TV. **Which leads many to the argument that London fashion is, by definition, cooler, because being cool means not caring too much, or not looking too much as if you care, and with all respect to my adopted city, New York evidently cares a lot and all the time.** On the other hand, never-not-caring can result, in New York, in the sort of avant-garde sensibility you see less of in London, especially among the very old. In London, to be very old and still caring about clothes is to be 'eccentric', dressed in many colours, perhaps, or with one's hair coloured in some unlikely, spirited way, and bright red glasses and 'jolly' accessories and so on. But I quite often see 80-year-olds in New York dressed in asymmetric all-black fashion sourced from obscure Japanese labels, or wearing hard-to-comprehend shoes that look like installation art, and with their hair tied back in a severe grey braid that reaches down to the waist or else shaved off completely — all without a hint of whimsy. Gives me hope.

Some New York memos, collective and unindividuated and everywhere, are simultaneously signs of widespread social transformation, and therefore heartening to see. Afro hair worn natural, boys in sequins and eyeshadow, gender-neutral separates. Others drive me to distraction. For three winters in a row, I swear there wasn't a woman in New York who didn't own a ribbed woollen hat with a fake-fur bobble on it (although when

I emailed friends in London, it sounded as if it was just as bad over there). And last fall, the ubiquity of teddy bear coats made me feel violent towards teddy bears, as a breed. This tendency towards conformity is most visible at black-tie events, where previously reasonable New York women suddenly unleash their inner prom queen en masse. And when everyone's in a strapless satin gown, it isn't very hard for a Londoner in a jumpsuit to imagine herself some kind of fashion radical. (In London itself, you'd have to work a lot bloody harder.)

When it comes to nostalgia or historical dressing (another form of memo), I'd say London has the edge, having so much more history to draw from. You'd look peculiar in Pilgrim-era wear in America, but a high-necked Queen Anne-style dress can still make sense back home. The '50s, '60s, '70s and '80s are regularly mined on the London high streets, whereas in New York, for the moment, the '90s is all there is. Part of the issue with American clothes nostalgia is surely that every era, if you think about it for half a second, was fun for the few and hell for the many. Last Christmas I was invited to a Mad Men-era costume party. Not wanting to arrive chained to a lunch counter, I racked my brains for something glamorous and ended up going for 'Diahann Carroll at a Hollywood party in Malibu', only to discover that every other black person at the party had gone as a Panther, black beret and all. A spectacular case of missing the memo.

That was a true fashion disaster, but I make more of them in London. So much socialising there is done indoors, in houses and flats, and it's very easy to be overdressed in someone's living room. Personally, I think it passive aggressive to ask someone to dinner then answer the door barefoot in sweatpants, but maybe that's just me. I'm also conscious of overdressing for a night on the town, forgetting the hard-won realism that leads London clubbers to think very carefully about what they truly want to be wearing at 3am, miles from home, pissed, looking down the barrel of a long night-bus journey. Athleisure is a transatlantic malady, but more people seem inclined to wear it all day in New York than in London, and unless you want people to roll their eyes at you and accuse you of being 'so New York', best not wear leggings after midday.

Behind my own front door, left to my own devices, it's some version of pyjamas all day long, no matter where I am. To write, I have to feel absolutely unhindered by elastic, buttons, cuffs, collars, belts, socks, laces, zips. Old Mets sweatshirt. Unspeakable, threadbare NYU tracksuit bottoms. Woolly beanie. It's a 'look' that depresses everyone I live with, but I can't manage any other way. Clothes, to me, are performance, and I like participating up to a point – but only up to a point. I never get tired of watching others, though. The streets of New York and London are the best shows I know, and nothing pleases me more than watching the people go by, their fascinating or outré or banal or bizarre self-conceptions made visible in fabric. 'Vain trifles as they seem, clothes have, they say, more important offices than to merely keep us warm. They change our view of the world and the world's view of us.' Woolf again. She was even more conflicted about clothes than I am, but she better understood that what a woman does with her wardrobe is not very different from what a novelist does with her characters: clothing the self as a way of viewing the world and of being viewed. My own truest self-conception in clothes – pyjamas – is of course best kept off the streets, but if I ever do feel like going out that way, in a pair of furry slides, to seize the day in the clothes I just slept in, well, there's always LA.

OSCAR WILDE
on Proportions

Wilde, a supporter of the Rational Dress Society, of which his wife was a founding member, wrote 'The Philosophy of Dress' for the *New York Tribune* in 1885. The essay was rediscovered in 2012 and published for the first time in book form in 2013.

THERE HAS BEEN WITHIN THE last few years, both in America and in England, a marked development of artistic taste. It is impossible to go into the houses of any of our friends without seeing at once that a great change has taken place. There is a far greater feeling for color, a far greater feeling for the delicacy of form, as well as a sense that art can touch the commonest things of the household into a certain grace and a certain loveliness. But there is also a whole side of the human life which has been left almost entirely untouched. I mean of course the dress of men and of women . . .

I have been sometimes accused of setting too high an importance on dress. To this I answer that dress in itself is a thing to me absolutely unimportant. In fact the more complete a dress looks on the dummy-figure of the milliner's shop, the less suitable it is for being worn. The gorgeous costumes of M. Worth's *atelier* seems to me like those Capo di Monte cups, which are all curves and coralhandles, and covered over with a Pantheon of gods and goddesses in high excitement and higher relief; that is to say, they are curious things to look at, but entirely unfit for use. The French milliners consider that women are created specially for them by Providence, in order to display their elaborate and expensive wares. I hold that dress is made for the

67

service of Humanity. They think that Beauty is a matter of frills and furbelows. I care nothing at all for frills, and I don't know what furbelows are, but I care a great deal for the wonder and grace of the human Form, and I hold that the very first canon of art is that Beauty is always organic, and comes from within, and not from without, comes from the perfection of its own being and not from any added prettiness. And that consequently the beauty of a dress depends entirely and absolutely on the loveliness it shields, and on the freedom and motion that it does not impede.

From this it follows that there can be no beauty of national costume until there is a national knowledge of the proportions of the human form. To Greek and Roman such knowledge came naturally from the gymnasium and the palaestra, from the dance in the meadow and the race by the stream. We must acquire it by the employment of art in education. And knowledge of the kind I propose would soon become the inheritance of all, if each child were taught to draw as early as it is taught to write . . .

And if a child does study the human figure it will learn a great many valuable laws of dress. It will learn, for instance, that a waist is a very beautiful and delicate curve, the more delicate the more beautiful, and not, as the milliner fondly imagines, an abrupt right angle suddenly occurring in the middle of the person. He will learn again that size has nothing to do with beauty. This, I dare say, seems a very obvious proposition. So it is. All truths are perfectly obvious once one sees them. The only thing is to see them. Size is a mere accident of existence, it is not a quality of Beauty ever. A great cathedral is beautiful, but so is the bird that flies round its pinnacle, and the butterfly that settles on its shaft. A foot is not necessarily beautiful because it is small. The smallest feet in the world are those of the Chinese ladies, and they are the ugliest also.

It is curious that so many people, while they are quite ready to recognize, in looking at an ordinary drawing-room, that the horizontal line of frieze and dado diminishes the height of the room, and the vertical lines of pillar or panel increase it, yet should not see that the same laws apply to dress also. Indeed in modern costume the horizontal line is used far too often, the vertical line far too rarely, and the oblique line scarcely at all.

The waist, for instance, is as a rule placed too low down. A long waist implies a short skirt, which is always ungraceful as it conveys an effect of short limbs, whereas a high waist gives an opportunity of a fine series of vertical lines falling in the folds of the dress down to the feet, and giving a sense of tallness and grace. Broad puffed sleeves, again, by intensifying the horizontal line across the shoulders, may be worn by those that are tall and slight, as they diminish any excessive height and give proportion; by those who are small they should be avoided. And the oblique line, which one gets by a cloak falling from the shoulder across the body, or by a gown looped up at the side, is suitable to almost all figures. It is a line which corresponds to the direction of motion, and conveys an impression of dignity as well as of freedom.

There are of course many other applications of these lines. I have mentioned merely one or two in order to remind people how identical the laws of architecture and of dress really are, and how much depends on line and proportion. Indeed the test of a good costume is its silhouette, how, in fact, it would look in sculpture.

But besides line there is also colour. In decorating a room, unless one wants the room to be either chaos or a museum, one must be quite certain of one's color-scheme. So also in dress. The harmony of color must be clearly settled. If one is small the simplicity of one color has many advantages. If one is taller two colors or three may be used. I do not wish to give a purely arithmetical basis for an aesthetic question, but perhaps three shades of color are the limit. At any rate it should be remembered that in looking at any beautifully dressed person, the eye should be attracted by the loveliness of line and proportion, and the dress should appear a complete harmony from the head to the feet; and that the sudden appearance of any violent contrasting color, in bow or riband, distracts the eye from the dignity of the ensemble, and concentrates it on a mere detail.

Then as regards the kind of colors, I should like to state once for all there is no such thing as a specially artistic color. All good colors are equally beautiful; it is only in the question of their combination that art comes in. And one should have no more preference for one color over another than one has for one note on the piano over its neighbor. Nor are there any sad colors. There are bad colors, such as Albert blue, and magenta, and arsenic green, and the colors of aniline dyes generally, but a good color always gives one pleasure. And the tertiary and secondary colors are for general use the safest, as they do not show wear easily, and besides give one a sense of repose and quiet. A dress should not be like a steam whistle, for all that M. Worth may say.

Then as regards pattern. It should not be too definite. **A strong marked check, for instance, has many disadvantages.** To begin with, it makes the slightest inequality in the figure, such as between the two shoulders, very apparent; then it is difficult to join the pattern accurately at the seams; and lastly, it distracts the eye away from the proportions of the figure, and gives the mere details an abnormal importance.

Then, again, the pattern should not be too big. I mention this, because I happened lately in London to be looking for some stamped gray plush or velvet, suitable for making a cloak of. Every shop that I went into the man showed me the most enormous patterns, things far too big for an ordinary wallpaper, far too big for ordinary curtains, things, in fact, that would require a large public building to show them off to any advantage. I entreated the shopman to show me a pattern that would be in some rational and relative proportion to the figure of somebody who was not over ten or twelve feet in height. He replied that he was extremely sorry but it was impossible; the smaller patterns were no longer being woven, in fact, the big patterns were in fashion. Now when he said the word fashion, he mentioned what is the great enemy of art in this century, as in all centuries. Fashion rests upon folly. Art rests upon law. Fashion is ephemeral. Art is eternal. Indeed what is a fashion really? **A fashion is merely a form of ugliness so absolutely unbearable that we have to alter it every six months!** It is quite clear that were it beautiful and rational we would not alter anything that combined those two rare qualities. And wherever dress has been so, it has remained unchanged in law and principle for many hundred years. And if any of my practical friends in the States refuse to recognize the value of the permanence of artistic laws, I am quite ready to rest the point entirely on an economic basis. The amount of money that is spent every year in America on dress is something almost fabulous. I have no desire to weary my readers with statistics, but if I were to state the sum that is spent yearly on bonnets alone, I am sure that one-half of the community would be filled with remorse and the other half with despair! So I will content myself with saying that it is something quite out of proportion to the splendor of modern dress, and that its reason must be looked for, not in the magnificence of the apparel, but rather in that unhealthy necessity for change which Fashion imposes on its beautiful and misguided votaries.

I am told, and I am afraid that I believe it, that if a person has recklessly invested in what is called 'the latest Paris bonnet,' and worn it to the rage and jealousy of the neighborhood for a fortnight, her dearest friend is quite certain to call upon her, and to mention incidentally that that particular kind of bonnet has gone entirely out of fashion. Consequently a new bonnet has at once to be bought, that Fifth Ave. may be appeased, and more expense entered into. Whereas were the laws of dress founded on art instead of on fashion, there would be no necessity for this constant evolution of horror from horror. What is beautiful looks always new and always delightful, and can no more become old-fashioned than a flower can. Fashion, again, is reckless of the individuality of her worshippers, cares nothing whether they be tall or short, fair or dark, stately or slight, but bids them all be attired exactly in the same way, until she can invent some new wickedness. Whereas Art permits, nay even ordains to each, that perfect liberty which comes from obedience to law, and which is something far better for humanity than the tyranny of tight lacing or the anarchy of aniline dyes.

And now as regards the cut of the dress.

The first and last rule is this, that each separate article of apparel is to be suspended from the shoulders always, and never from the waist. Nature, it should be noted, gives one no opportunity at all of suspending anything from the waist's delicate curve. Consequently by means of a tight corset a regular artificial ledge has to be produced, from which the lower garment may be securely hung. Where there are petticoats, there must be corsets. Annihilate the former and the latter disappear. And I have no hesitation in saying that whenever in history we find that dress has become absolutely monstrous and ugly, it has been partly of course through the mistaken idea that dress has an independent existence of its own, but partly also through the fashion of hanging the lower garments from the waist. In the sixteenth century, for instance, to give the necessary compression, Catherine d'Medici, High Priestess of poison and petticoats, invented a corset which may be regarded as the climax of a career of crime. It was made of steel, had a front and a back to it like the cuirass of a fire-brigade man, and was secured under the left arm by a hasp and pin, like a Saratoga trunk. Its object was to diminish the circumference of the waist to a circle of thirteen inches, which was the fashionable size without which a lady was not allowed to appear at court; and its influence on the health and beauty of the age may be estimated by the fact that the normal waist of a well-grown woman is an oval of twenty-six to twenty-eight inches certainly.

As one bad habit always breeds another, in order to support the weight of the petticoats the fardingale was invented also. This was a huge structure, sometimes of wickerwork like a large clothes-basket, sometimes of steel ribs, and extended on each side to such an extent that in the reign of Elizabeth an English lady in full dress took up quite as much room as we would give now to a very good sized political meeting. I need hardly point out what a selfish fashion this was, considering the limited surface of the globe. Then in the last century there was the hoop, and in this the crinoline. But, I will be told, ladies have long ago given up crinoline, hoop and fardingale. That is so. And I am sure we all feel very grateful to them. I certainly do. Still, does there not linger, even now, amongst us that dreadful, that wicked thing, called the Dress-Improver? Is not that vilest of all diminutives, the crinolette, still to be seen! I am quite sure that none of my readers ever dream of wearing anything of the kind. But there may be others who are not so wise, and I wish it could be conveyed to them, delicately and courteously, that the hourglass is not the ideal of Form. Often a modern dress begins extremely well. From the neck to the waist the lines of the dress itself follow out with more or less completeness the lines of the figure; but the lower part of the costume becomes bell shaped and heavy, and breaks out into a series of harsh angles and coarse curves. Whereas if from the shoulders, and the shoulders only, each separate article were hung, there would be then no necessity for any artificial supports of the kind I have alluded to, and tight lacing could be done away with. If some support is considered necessary, as it often is, a broad woollen band, or band of elastic webbing, held up by shoulder straps, would be found quite sufficient.

So much on the cut of the dress, now for its decoration.

The French milliner passes a lurid and lucrative existence in sewing on bows where there should be no bows, and flounces where there should be no flounces. But, alas! his industry is in vain. For all ready-made ornamentation merely makes a dress ugly to look at and cumbersome to wear. **The beauty of dress, as the beauty of life, comes always from freedom.** At every moment a dress should respond to the play of the girl who wears it, and exquisitely echo the melody of each movement and each gesture's grace. Its loveliness is to be sought for in the delicate play of light and line in dainty rippling folds and not in the useless ugliness and ugly uselessness of a stiff and stereotyped decoration. It is true that in many of the latest Paris dresses which I have seen there seems to be some recognition of the value of folds. But unfortunately the folds are all artificially made and sewn down, and so their charm is entirely destroyed. For a fold in a dress is not a fact, an item to be entered in a bill, but a certain effect of light and shade which is only exquisite because it is evanescent. Indeed one might just as well paint a shadow on a dress as sew a fold down on one. And the chief reason that a modern dress wears such a short time is that it cannot be smoothed out, as a dress should be, when it is laid aside in the wardrobe. In fact in a fashionable dress there is far too much 'shaping'; the very wealthy of course will not care, but it is worthwhile to remind those who are not millionaires that the more seams the more shabbiness. A well-made dress should last almost as long as a shawl, and if it is well made it does. And what I mean by a well-made dress is a simple dress that hangs from the shoulders, that takes its shape from the figure and its folds from the movements of the girl who wears it, and what I mean by a badly made dress is an elaborate structure of heterogeneous materials, which having been first cut to pieces with the shears, and then sewn together by the machine, are ultimately so covered with frills and bows and flounces as to become execrable to look at, expensive to pay for, and absolutely useless to wear.

Well, these are the principles of Dress. And probably it will be said that all these principles might be carried out to perfection, and yet no definite style be the result. Quite so. With a definite style, in the sense of a historical style, we have nothing

Style and Substance

whatsoever to do. There must be no attempt to revive an ancient mode of apparel simply because it is ancient, or to turn life into that chaos of costume, the Fancy Dress Ball. We start, not from History, but from the proportions of the human form. Our aim is not archaeological accuracy, but the highest possible amount of freedom with the most equable distribution of warmth. And the question of warmth brings me to my last point. It has some-times been said to me, not by the Philistine merely but by artistic people who are really interested in the possibility of a beautiful dress, that the cold climate of Northern countries necessitates our wearing so many garments, one over the other, that it is quite impossible for dress to follow out or express the lines of the figure at all. This objection, however, which at first sight may seem to be a reasonable one, is in reality founded on a wrong idea, on the idea in fact that the warmth of apparel depends on the number of garments worn. Now the weight of apparel depends very much on the number of garments worn, but the warmth of apparel depends entirely on the material of which those garments are made. And one of the chief errors in modern costume comes from the particular material which is always selected as the basis for dress. We have always used linen, whereas the proper mat-erial is wool. Wool, to begin with, is a nonconductor of heat. That means that in the summer the violent heat of the sun does not enter and scorch the body, and that the body in winter remains at its normal natural temperature, and does not waste its vital warmth on the air. Those of my readers who play lawn tennis and like outdoor sports know that, if they wear a complete flannel suit, they are perfectly cool on the hottest day, and perfectly warm when the day is cold. All that I claim is that the same laws which are clearly recognized on the tennis ground, flannel being a woollen texture, should be recognized as being equally suitable for the dress of people who live in towns, and whose lives are often necessarily sedentary. There are many other qualities in wool, such as its being an absorber and distributor of moisture, with regard to which I would like to refer my readers to a little handbook on 'Health Culture,' by Dr. Jaeger the Professor of Physiology at Stuttgart. Dr. Jaeger does not enter into the question of form or beauty, at least when he does he hardly seems to me very successful, but on the sanitary values of different textures and colours he speaks of course with authority, and from a combination of the principles of science with the laws of art will come, I feel sure, the costume of the future.

For if wool is selected as the basis and chief material of dress, far fewer garments may be worn than at present, with the result of immensely increased warmth and much greater lightness and comfort. Wool also has the advantage of being almost the most delicate texture woven. Silk is often coarse compared to it, being at once harder and colder. A large cashmere shawl of pure wool can be drawn through a tiny ring, indeed by this method do the shawlsellers of the Eastern bazaar show to one the fineness of their goods. Wool, again, shows no creases. I should be sorry to see such a lovely texture as satin disappear from modern dress, but every lady who wears anything of the kind knows but too well how easily it crumples; besides it is better to wear a soft than hard material, for in the latter there is always a danger of harsh and coarse lines, whereas in the former you get the most exquisite delicacy of fold.

We find, then, that on the question of material Science and Art are one. And as regards the milliners' method of dress I would like to make one last observation. Their whole system is not merely ugly but useless. It is of no avail that a stately lady pinches in her waist in order to look slight. For size is a question of proportion. And an unnaturally small waist merely makes the shoulders look abnormally broad and heavy. The high heel, again, by placing the foot at a sharp angle bends the figure forward, and thus so far from giving any additional height, robs it of at least an inch and a half. People who can't stand straight must not imagine that they look tall. Nor does the wearing of a lofty headdress improve the matter. Its effect is merely to make the head disproportionately large. A dwarf three feet high with a hat of six cubits on his head will look a dwarf three feet high to the end. Indeed height is to be measured more by the position of the eyes and the shoulders than by anything else. And particular care should be taken not to make the head too large. Its perfect proportion is one-eighth of the whole figure . . .

But I know that, irrespective of Congress, the women of America can carry any reform they like. And I feel certain that they will not continue much longer to encourage a style of dress which is founded on the idea that the human figure is deformed and requires the devices of the milliner to be made presentable. For have they not the most delicate and dainty hands and feet in the world? Have they not complexions like ivory stained with a roseleaf? Are they not always in office in their own country, and do they not spread havoc through Europe?

HARRY LAMBERT
on Playfulness

Super-stylist to a small group of stars in music, sport and film, Harry Lambert is the man who put Harry Styles in a Gucci pussy-bow blouse and single pearl earring for the Met Gala, transforming him into one of contemporary pop music's most memorable dressers. Harry is committed to creating pop culture moments. And having fun. Lots and lots of fashion fun.

I DON'T HAVE A VERY intellectual approach to style or a deep knowledge of fashion. I came to it relatively late by industry standards, by which I mean aged twenty, when I finished my photography studies and realised that what I really wanted was to be a stylist.

I didn't grow up in a world where anybody knew about Gucci or Prada or Givenchy. I was always obsessed with what I was wearing but it wasn't as if I read *Vogue* every month. I just loved clothes, and I mostly experienced them through pop culture. I watched Madonna and Britney Spears videos, and as I got more into music I discovered Prince and Bowie and the Stones and Elvis. I noticed that the impact of these musicians was heightened by what outfits they wore when they performed, whether it was Madonna wearing a Jean Paul Gaultier conical-cup corset for the Blond Ambition tour or Prince in a frilly white blouse and purple suit in *Purple Rain*. That's what I've always wanted to do: make outfits that the people who are wearing them will enjoy and the people who are watching will remember.

I think fandom is brilliant. It can be a real spur to creativity. Taylor Swift's fans post TikTok videos of themselves getting ready

Style and Substance

78

to go to see her, where they customise their clothes with elements from her stage outfits. At Harry [Styles]'s shows, people make their own clothes and everyone wears a feather boa . . . I love it when somebody dresses up as him for a party because that means we've been noticed and adopted as part of a repertoire of playful looks that others can draw on. If the images we create contribute to a conversation about gender in fashion, say, then I'm pleased but that's never my motivation. All I set out to do is inspire people to have fun and create memorable looks. The irony is that sometimes that's enough to conjure up moments that go on to contribute to the political conversation of the times. But that's almost nothing to do with me. It's just that fashion is powerful.

I find it way harder to dress myself than to dress other people, but I have developed a bit of a look, I suppose. I always wear a big necklace. I can't get dressed without one these days; they've become almost a safety blanket. I have a lot from a brand called éliou based in Miami who made loads for Harry Styles and for me, in different colours. Very simple, with large shiny beads. I recently bought an old Balenciaga crystal choker . . . I go through phases of wearing a particular necklace and then move on to something else. When I started wearing a pearl necklace about five years ago, people would stare or stop me in the street to ask me about it. Things have changed a lot since then. Now a necklace on a man no longer even signifies sexuality; it's just something that boys who are into fashion do. It's quite nonchalant.

As well as the necklaces, I love a statement shirt and I wear a lot of T-shirts with silly characters on them. I consider myself a happy person, so it comes naturally to me. Plus, when you're having fun with clothes, it's welcoming to other people. When I started as an intern at *i-D* and *Vogue*, I found the fashion world sometimes took itself quite seriously which could be a bit intimidating. So, for me, a sense of fun is important to break down people's anxieties about style, my own included! I'm currently obsessed with some JW Anderson slippers he's made with

Wellipets, which are like giant frogs on your feet. I wear them on set. If people don't get it, that's fun too.

When my team and I are enjoying ourselves at work, everything feels easy and possibilities open up. I've noticed this most recently with Emma Corrin. We've explored a lot of playful looks and that builds our mutual confidence, which in turn makes her feel more daring. For the premiere of *My Policeman*, we decided she would wear a mini dress by JW Anderson that looked like a goldfish in a plastic bag. I love the way that playfulness can lead to more experimentation. Sometimes the outfits end up being almost avant-garde but it's all based on silliness rather than grand ideas.

I'm really interested in transformation. Photographer Cindy Sherman's self-portraits as imagined characters were a big inspiration for me and have definitely influenced my styling work. I enjoy surrealism. Theatricality in general is part of the mix. I went to drama classes at the local theatre school in Norwich between the ages of seven and eighteen and have always been fascinated by costume. I often visit costume archives in search of ideas. But, as I say, my approach is intuitive rather than based on deep immersion in fashion history.

Is there such a thing as too much? Definitely. You always need a wild card option when you're putting together a look, but you need to know when to use it and when to decide against. I remember one time when I was styling Eddie Redmayne for a big event, in collaboration with Gucci. They wanted him to wear a red mesh crystal top. I wasn't at all convinced but we tried it and it ended up being perfect; he completely owned it. On other occasions, with other people, the wild cards just haven't worked. Which is fine. It's good to try things out.

Being able to edit a look is crucial. You can't keep adding more and more of anything without eventually crossing the fine line between fabulous and a mess. If you add one element too many, it tips into messy or ends up being too much like costume. Which I love, but only as inspo; not as a total outfit.

To be stylish, you really have to not care what other people think of what you're wearing. There's a contradiction at play because, of course, *you* need to care about your choices. To create an impact, people must notice you, which means you need to have thought about what you're wearing. You've got to build your own style DNA, figure out what's your vibe and what works for you. But the most stylish people have done all that; they just don't give a shit about your opinion of it! They have an energy of 'What? This is just what I'm wearing.' That's pure style.

The first piece I bought with my own money:

There are two that stick in my mind. I bought them around the same time. One was a Saint Laurent black-and-white Hawaiian shirt, the other was a Prada denim tunic top — they were the first two break-the-bank purchases that I had to deliberate over for days . . . I wore that shirt to death. It was made of crepe de chine and I wore a backpack in those days, so the back of the shirt ended up in tatters. I still have it in my studio in a drawer, in case the day comes when I need it.

The Prada denim top got too small for me and I sold it, but I think about it to this day. There's another stylist who still wears the one I really wanted that I couldn't afford. I'm so jealous.

The one piece I'd save if my home was on fire:

A pair of reconstructed jeans by JW Anderson from his second collection. They're Levi's cut up and remade. They're like Frankenstein jeans, stitched together with thick brown wool. He only made a couple of pairs and they were never for sale. They're the most fabulous jeans and I absolutely love them. I used to fit into them, maybe one day I will again!

81

PART 3

STYLE TRIBES

'It is from clothes that we form a first impression of our
fellow creatures as we meet them.'

J. C. FLÜGEL,
The Psychology of Clothes

'If the songs don't go over, we can do a medley of
costumes.'

ELVIS

MIQUITA OLIVER
on Caribbean Preppy Style

Miquita is a TV and radio broadcaster who shot to fame at the age of sixteen when she began co-hosting Channel 4's irreverent pop culture show, *Popworld*. She recently co-presented BBC2's *The Caribbean with Andi and Miquita*, alongside her mother. She has worked with Fashion Favours and Oxfam to promote the ethical and ecological benefits of circular fashion since 2008, and says that 'second-hand clothes shops are the most fun way I know to figure out who I am.'

I'M CONVINCED THAT STYLE CAN be inherited, passed down the generations like green eyes or big ears. On my mother's side I'm descended from generations of Caribbean people who made their own clothes, visited the tailors and believed that self-respect was expressed through dressing well. I have a photo of my grandma as a little girl, surrounded by her family in Antigua. She's sitting next to her mother, my great-grandma. Everyone's wearing their Sunday best: chic, simple clothes, cut beautifully. The women are in knee-length skirts and kitten heels, stripey short-sleeved skinny knitwear. The girls are in perfect little dresses, there are narrow trousers and crisp shirts for the boys. All the men are in slim tailoring. And the astounding thing about this for me is that my great-grandma made all her own clothes and all the children's clothes. My aunties made their own clothes, too. They look like they're in Chanel, the cuts are so sharp.

I've always been conscious of the style influence of the Black-British community I grew up in, around West London. The women wore neat separates every day and full skirted, waisted dresses for special occasions and church. They always looked groomed. The men wore a suit for church and for best and mixed sportswear for day-to-day, but the sportswear I saw my stepfather and his friends wearing in the late 1980s and 1990s was so carefully put together, it might as well have been tailoring. They wore really good Adidas tracksuit trousers with the stripes hanging perfectly straight and the hems just so, paired with a Polo shirt or a button-down cardigan and either immaculate trainers or Clarks shoes.

Elements from the British colonial culture people had known in the Caribbean, such as the Clarks shoes, the suits and brogues or the waisted dresses, were mixed in with newer styles they found in London, such as the sportswear. It was constantly evolving but always rooted in an almost preppy style of old-fashioned chic. The best example of this was my uncle Sean. He bought his suits from charity shops but he was from this family of makers, he had an eye. So he picked out the perfect shade of grey; the perfect cut. He made these charity shop suits look like Armani. Then he would wear them with mash-up Adidas trainers and the perfect hat or chain. It was just so cool. And so much fun.

Nobody in that community could afford to look scruffy. They were either first generation arrivals or the descendants of the Windrush generation. They'd come over to the UK imagining they were travelling to the motherland and found something much more complex. Many of them were treated terribly. The racism, discrimination, hostility and disrespect were constant. I grew up witnessing the way that my community used clothes as a way to assert their value, and their dogged optimism about the future. **It was about dressing for your dignity in the face of everything that was happening.**

I've been influenced by all of it. I love sportswear and vintage trainers, and I also love kitten heels and chic separates, especially short skirts. I'm not a dress person at all. To my mind, a dress is almost too easy. As a child I had a book of cut-out dolls with different outfits you could dress them in. I played for hours, trying out different combinations of blouse and slacks or sweater and skirt, with different shoes and accessories. That was my earliest training in putting a look together. It's still the way I think about outfits, very deliberately.

And yet, even knowing all this about the influence of my family and community, I still wasn't prepared for the realisation I had on my first visit to Antigua in 2021 when I met my extended family on that side. **You don't necessarily know how much of your style is inherited until you start looking into it.** You think to yourself, 'I just love a neat little jumper.' And then you look around and realise that all your aunties wear them. And your favourite outfit just happens to be a carefully cut miniskirt with perhaps a crisp Polo shirt, a short jacket and a kitten heel. The same classic shapes and classic pieces that generations of your family have worn.

Everyone chooses the clothes they put on for a reason. Style is sometimes about community, it can be a way to show that you belong to a particular group whose values you share, as it was for the Black West Londoners of my childhood and still is even now. I see uncles dressed in their tweed suit sitting at the bus stop on a Sunday in Ladbroke Grove or Hackney. It's like a uniform; it never drops.

Style is also so intimate and personal. It's about exploring yourself, moulding or disguising yourself. Clothes are tools. I've used them all my life, to build my confidence, get over heartbreak and expand my sense of who I can be. I've also used them to hide away or impersonate the person I thought I ought to be.

When I was twenty-eight, I started to go through a really tough time in my life. I'd been in broadcasting for twelve years by then and both my career and life had gone off the rails. It was never a tragedy but it was hard. I was scared. I gained a lot of weight, lost a lot of confidence and got into debt. I didn't recognise myself. I was a mess for a couple of years. Eventually I found my way through. I changed my lifestyle so I could lose the weight healthily. I started training every day and trying to figure out how to get my career straightened out. When I went back to broadcasting I was so delighted to be there, I decided to dress how I thought a TV presenter should look. I'd never used a stylist on *Popworld*, just worn whatever second-hand clothes I had in my wardrobe. Now I deferred to the TV executives. I was so grateful to be back. But even though some people might have said I'd never looked better – I was thin, I was wearing sleek little black dresses and my hair was long and straightened and glossy – I felt a very long way from myself. I had lost touch with my style inheritance – both the Caribbean preppy look and the second-hand clothes obsession. I wasn't dressing honestly. I was hiding, conforming. That phase didn't last too long because it just felt all wrong!

Later, when an important relationship ended and I was heartbroken just as we went into lockdown, I used clothes every day to remind myself who I was, to generate the strength to get out of bed and to protect myself from all the pain I was in. At a time when I could control so little and I was so hurt, I chose my outfits more carefully than ever. I would post what I was wearing on Instagram every day. Clothes kept bringing me back to who I really was. It was such a comfort. I started to have fun again. Getting dressed, being well dressed, was like medicine.

It wasn't about shopping. I wasn't diving into consumerism, buying ten blazers from Zara every week to kill my heartbreak. It was more like using the contents of my wardrobe to experiment and play, as I had played with those cut-out dolls as a child. Clothes kept bringing me back to who I really was. Your style is something that no one can take from you. **Even if everything else has been taken, or lost or damaged: your heart, your soul . . . You can still dress as the person you know yourself to be.**

This is why I love walking into a second-hand clothes shop:

because it's stuffed full of different ways to construct an identity for yourself. None of it has been designed to be this season's shape or print. It's not like a regular shop, where you can pick the same dress in one of three colourways. It's a melting pot of options. You are not being told what they have. You have to find it, by trusting your instincts and your gut, by exploring, taking a few risks, making mistakes. There's something so inspiring about having to really look to see what's there and then listen to your own voice in response. It's an act of personal affirmation.

I think it helps to have a combination of curiosity and intuition, and both those things can be practised. I've always been somebody who enjoys doing my research; you have to be, as a broadcaster. But really, I just notice clothes everywhere I look. Ever since I was a kid wandering around the market on Portobello Road back in the early nineties. I used to watch the people on the stalls, the locals sitting outside the cafes. There's inspiration everywhere. I was watching the Michelle Pfeiffer film *The Fabulous Baker Street Boys* the other day and now I really want to wear a simple stylish sexy red dress. That's not fashionable, but it's what I want to wear.

At the moment I'm inspired by Nina Simone, her incredible separates and her hair wraps, and by Bob Marley's mixed Caribbean-Scottish-influenced take on sportswear and narrow tailoring. That look really resonates for me because the other side of my inheritance is Scottish via my birth father. Scottish people like to dress with dignity too.

I'm also impressed and inspired by my mother's use of clothes as a tool of resistance to the process of being erased and ignored. This routinely happens to middle-aged women, especially middle-aged women of colour, especially those who don't use their hair as beauty. Watching what she's done over the last five years has been incredible. This is a woman who had absolutely no relationship with clothes for at least fifteen years. She was extremely overweight, going through midlife, and she did not care what she wore at all. She didn't think it was worth caring. Then she started losing weight and getting big jobs on television again. 'Take the stylist they're offering,' I said, somehow thinking that her situation was different from the self-same one I'd found myself in, a few years earlier. She refused. She set off on her own journey of reinventing herself through clothes and found her own style by listening to her own voice. She helped me to remember that this is vital, for everyone, and when the risks seem higher, the rewards will be that much sweeter. **So now she has this iconic look, and it has captivated people to see a woman in her late fifties dress like a fly motherfucker! Uncle Sean would have been so proud.**

M.I.A.
on Finding What Speaks to Her

She's the fearless, award-winning musician, artist and performer who pivoted from studying film to making some of the first underground music to be distributed and discovered online back in the early 2000s. She pioneered the high-lo fashion format in the music industry introducing a new approach that artists and singers continue to reference today. Twenty years later, she's still defying categorisation with her unique sound and still is a vision of cool. Her influence in fashion has yet to be measured.

I'M INSPIRED BY A MESOPOTAMIAN statue in the Metropolitan Museum of Art in New York, called 'Sumerian Standing Female Worshipper', from 2300 BC. The figure is wearing a saree, as South Asians do today. It's fascinating that a corner of fashion has remained the same for at least 4500 years.

One of my earliest memories is of learning to sew with my mum. She was a seamstress and I practically lived under her worktable, collecting the fabric she threw away. I made my first clothes out of patchwork scraps.

Growing up in London, my sister was a huge influence. As early teens we wore European streetwear brands like Chipie, NAF NAF, Chevignon and Benetton. We were both super into fashion and aspired to go to Central Saint Martins. We would hang out in Harvey Nicks after school, drooling over clothes. Our fashion designer uncle put us on to designers he liked by buying us perfumes. We were wearing Moschino and Versace at jungle raves in London in 1991 and 1992, before US rap blew it up. There was definitely an element of influence from NWA or Salt-N-Pepa.

At that time, before Lil' Kim's first LP or Junior Mafia or Biggie, all the cool East Coast people were dressing like Wu Tang and all the West Coast people dressed like NWA.

I have a bit of a refugee aesthetic, a mash up of all the eras and areas I've experienced. I've often dressed in what I could thrift, so whatever was being shipped via Oxfam to developing world countries. When we shot the videos for *Galang* or *Bad Girls*, luckily it was American sports hip hop tees from the eighties and nineties that were eBay-able or thrift-able. We also made lots of custom. I sometimes make my own graphic printed fabrics, create my own designs and pair them with things I get at 99c stores or that my friends give me. I like to be practical and in touch with the moment, find what speaks to me. I judge clothes on what they mean to me, rather than fashion world trends. I have very simple codes. Though, being Tamil, I also love gold!

When I'm performing, I take my everyday style and try to elevate it. My first performances were in tracksuits. Missy had her iconic Adidas; I got to wear Ashish's first ever collection, and that was *so* iconic. It was a match made in heaven as his Aesthetic was exactly like mine but sequin-coated. Wearing a sequined Oxfam tee or sequined batik fabric tracksuit was like having your prayers answered. I loved wearing a Ralph Lauren polo with shorts and trainers in the council flat, then wearing the exact same look but a sequined version for stage.

Style is personal. It's a sense of self. Not lifted, not gifted but lived.

The one piece I'd save if my home was on fire:

The one-off, electric-blue sheepskin jacket Luella [Bartley] custom made with Bottega Veneta in around 2000 or 2001, when we lived together. I wore it in the videos for *Paper Planes* and *DBT*. It reminds me of the journey, and it's symbolic of the experimental and rule-breaking work we were all trying to do at the time.

DAPHNE GUINNESS
on Happy Accidents

One of the most recognisable and idiosyncratic figures on the fashion scene, Daphne has been a muse, a model and is now a musician. She collects haute couture and after the death of her great friend, Isabella Blow, she acquired Isabella's entire collection to preserve it as a resource for future fashion students. From her exquisite taste in millinery to her notorious 'heel-less' high heels, there's nobody else like Daphne Guinness.

WHEN I WAS YOUNGER, I really didn't stand out in terms of what I wore. Perhaps I've become less conventional in my style choices over time but another factor, at least as important in my view, is that the world has become more conservative around me. There were so many peacock tribes during the 1980s and 1990s, and I learned from them how I wanted to dress. I grew up in an analogue world where peer groups defined ourselves according to the music we listened to and the books and films and artists we liked. Style was a collaborative effort; we fed off each other's decisions and choices. I think that fostered a deeper sense of connection between members of style tribes, as well as more daring and creativity. The range of fashion inspiration online is a double-edged sword in my view. I missed the rise of smartphones because I went to live in the middle of nowhere in Ireland in 2011 and spent the next seven years focused on making and recording music. Life was very different when I came back.

My tribe is still that merry band of artists. We create music and art and style all together. And as the world has become more corporate and homogenised, I've just carried on doing my thing.

93

I've enjoyed dressing up ever since I was a child. These days it's just on a bigger scale.

I'm quite shy, so I use clothes as a defence and as a way to start the conversation I want to have. I dread going out, especially to parties, even though I have a good time once I get there. So I choose an outfit that will make me feel confident at that particular event. For everyday dressing when I'm working in the studio, I have more of a uniform. I don't want to think about what I'm wearing; I just want to feel fresh and ready to work. I wear a lot of black, or black and white.

Certain things about my look have become almost personal trademarks. The heel-less shoes, for example, or my two-colour hair, but both began as accidents rather than decisions. The shoes were a literal mishap. I was on a fashion shoot up a mountain when a heel broke off the shoe I was wearing. We hadn't finished shooting so I found some putty to make a replacement heel that allowed me to climb the slope and then removed it for more photos to be taken. I found this unexpectedly comfortable so I found somebody who could make heel-less shoes for me. I'm double jointed and they help to stretch my back out. It feels normal to me 'on set' though I know it looks odd to people on the outside.

My black and white hair was also an accident. I've always had very long hair, and as a fashion model it was dyed every colour you can imagine. At one point it was three different colours and almost down to my waist. Then a stylist decided to cut it very short and dye it black. I wasn't convinced but I went along with it, trying to be professional. Let's just say it wasn't a good look! It took about five years to grow long again. I couldn't face too many more decisions or risks, so after that I just went for baby blonde at the front and dark at the back.

I wear it in a backcombed 'up do' that accentuates my head, which has always seemed to me disproportionately large for my body. I'm short and very slim. I've got a tiny frame and then this enormous head! I like to play around with proportions and accentuate those parts of myself that are slightly odd. So the hairstyle came about because I wanted to elongate my head backwards, like an Egyptian goddess.

I've been very influenced by Chinese and Japanese costume. My great-great-grandfather was a diplomat in China and Japan and collected pieces that I loved as a child. I started collecting myself and have been privileged to be able to buy many wonderful things. I have Japanese kimonos from the 1930s that were influenced by European Surrealism. The colours are absolutely sublime. When I'm travelling I use them as decoration to brighten up bland hotel rooms. Sometimes I think they should be in museums but I just love wearing them too much. I love the storytelling, the grades of silk, the craftsmanship, the colours.

I look back to certain historical moments and movements for inspiration. I'm very drawn to a dark Byronesque Romantic take on menswear, for example. I love to wear dark tailcoats and jet-trimmed capes, clothes that conjure up a dark and mysterious feeling that suggests a blurring of masculine and feminine energy. I think I respond to that same ambiguity in clothes from the French courts of the seventeenth and eighteenth centuries, from Louis XIV to Louis XVI. That look is very different, far more colourful and extravagant, but there's a similar blurring between men's and women's wear. Then there's the old-fashioned glamour of 1930s and 1940s Hollywood, Hedy Lamarr and Billy Wilder's movies.

And music of course, which has always inspired me. When I was seven or eight it was glam rock and I used to watch Marc Bolan's TV show, *Marc*. Then there were The Doors, The Beatles, Bowie. The only time I'm not listening to music is when I'm depressed. Music helps me get dressed, get in the flow and put outfits together. I pull everything out on my bed and then I just gravitate towards things. When I'm singing, I wear pageboy tailcoats and long white shirts, shorts and tights and bodysuits, lots of ribbons and sparkles.

I consider all the elements of an outfit. I love millinery, shoes, jewellery, accessories, and I am theatrical. I am unafraid. That said, I am not an out and out maximalist. I think there is such a thing as too much, and sometimes that's a question of practicality rather than elegance. I always ask myself, 'Can you get out of it at the end of the night?' Too many layers and you're liable to get in a tangle. I put on as much as I can, and then start taking things off.

I've worn some extraordinary clothes in my time. It's very hard to pick out a favourite outfit. Perhaps one of my sequined coats . . . I love a sequin, they make me happy. Who are the coats by? Well, me I suppose; though they were made in the Chanel atelier. Karl used to say that he always knew where I was at a party. He could follow my trail because I left feathers and sequins in my wake. Or perhaps I would choose a kimono, a swimming suit, a good pair of shoes and lots of scarves. That's one of my favourite outfits.

SEBASTIAN HORSLEY
on Self-Invention

Artist, addict, male escort and brothel connoisseur, Sebastian Horsley chronicled his search for happiness, meaning and a good outfit in *Dandy in the Underworld*, which the *Sunday Times* called 'one of the funniest, strangest and most revolting memoirs every written'.

I SET ABOUT ANNOUNCING MYSELF as a dandy with renewed vigour, borrowing quite a lot from the wardrobe of the Regency. The period had always interested me. It was an era which had swung between extreme elegance and sodden brutality, an age of excess and exoticism, when the ruling class blazed, cracked and fizzed in a torrid Indian summer before the dismal winter of democracy descended. Rakes, strumpets, gamblers, murderers, drunkards and artists. Here was a devil-may-care individuality. Gentlemen were having their shoelaces ironed while half-naked children were sweeping their chimneys. Wilberforce was denouncing the slave trade while Beau Brummell was denouncing an imperfect cravat.

Mr Brummell was the original and most celebrated dandy but he was no hero of mine. He was so refined that I do not regard him as a dandy at all. I am more concerned with style than breeding. And the key is to dress in such a style that you would attract attention at a Liberace concert.

When it comes to dress, it takes a strong man to be an extrovert. A true dandy needs a complete conviction that he is right; the views of the rest of the world simply don't matter. 'If someone looks at you, you are not well dressed,' Mr Brummell tells us. But then Mr Brummell would say that; prissily precise, he was essentially a conformist. True dandyism is rebellious. The real dandy wants to make people look, be shocked by, and even a little scared by the subversion which his clothes stand for.

And yet, dandyism is social, human and intellectual. It is not a suit of clothes walking about by itself. Clothes are merely a part – they may even be the least important part of the personality of the dandy. Dandyism isn't image encrusted with flourishes. It's a way of stripping yourself down to your true self. You can only judge the style by the content and you can only reach the content through the style.

Being a dandy is a condition rather than a profession. It is a defence against suffering and a celebration of life. It is not fashion, it is not wealth, it is not learning, it is not beauty. It is a shield and a sword and a crown – all pulled out of the dressing up box in the attic of the imagination. **Dandyism is a lie which reveals the truth and the truth is that we are what we pretend to be.**

My immediate concern was: where in Edinburgh a pink suit had had the power to make even the most affable yob hurl his fish supper after me – in London it was merely accepted. I was standing around on street corners causing no sensation whatso-ever.

This would not do. A man with no talent must have a tailor. I selected from the most exclusive list: Mr Khan of Huntsman fame (and offensive flattery – I hold him personally responsible for the daffodil gabardine and the prawn cocktail pink suede. If I could get the money back from him, I would spend it on suing him for defamation of the characterless); Mr Powell, the Soho spiv; Mr Pearse, the Soho snob, oh, and Mr Eddie, the cut-price version for leisure wear.

Shopping list in head (and hole in my pocket), I set off on my spree.

Suits: sixty-nine (you need to be prepared for all permuta-tions).

Fabrics, I wanted to try out the cut (single-breasted, double-breasted, big-breasted, drape jacket, box jacket, straightjacket) of every cloth (except corduroy, of course). Wool, silk, cashmere, felt; suede, gabardine, worsted, tweed, velvet, mohair, pussyfur, bunnyfluff, moleskin, sharkskin, swansdown, eiderdown, seersucker, cocksucker etc. etc.

Good. Now for colours and patterns: herringbone, houndstooth, dogtooth, tartan, chalk stripe, pinstripe, Prince of Wales, Prince of Darkness, dot, spot, polka dot, plonker or what?

Black: jet black, inky black, ebony black, and drug-dealer black.

White: only in velvet and with a nacreous sheen.

Blue: sky-blue, cobalt, peacock and big cock.

Green: I don't go to the country.

Purple: Imperial, amethyst and mauve with lilac stitching.

Orange: I can't remember — even I never wore it.

Yellow: Primrose, crocus, daffodil and sunflower.

Red: Scarlet, cardinal, crimson, cinnabar; blood red, sin red, shoot-the-red, light red, great big fucking flag of danger red.

Pink: Soft pink, hard pink, petal pink, shell pink, shocking pink, even more shocking pink, flamingo pink, salmon pink, prawn-cocktail pink, spam pink. In the pink pink.

And that — even with a mutiny of shimmering satin linings to select from — was just a start.

There were coats — with their cuts and their plunges, their sweeps and their collars. (I found the Vicuna particularly satisfactory, though the wolfskin combined with tight astrakhan curls — from the fleece of an aborted baby lamb — made an appropriately queasy combination.) There were ties — handmade of course and always gratifyingly expensive — even when I started to wear them round my arm instead of my neck. There were scarves. My favourite was the rabbit, but I'd don any fur. An animal should be delicious and fit well. There were socks (if you haven't got any you can't pull them up), and they came in an impudence of colours and endless materials to match the climate and were all

99

monogrammed, just in case I forgot who I was. And of course there were shoes. I made straight for Lobbs, famously the finest makers of footwear in the world. Everyone who is anyone – or else absolutely loaded – goes there for brogues. How pointlessly boring. I commissioned a pair of Paul Stanley-style high-altitude platforms. Swaying and swanking across the shop floor in my stout, black-calf knee-high leather creations with their seven-inch heels, I attained six foot nine. I was well worth the climb. Such height lends a spurious air of nobility. But – oh God! – why such rare restraint. I commissioned only a single pair – at a cost of four grand.

Gloves. It was time for some real sartorial terrorism. Time to hurl the hand grenades. Women think that it's shoes that set off an outfit. But I don't pay much attention to womanish matters, except of course when it comes to gloves. And it's ladies gloves I like most – the softest kidskin with fur trims and silk linings, buttons at the wrist or little encircling puffs of fluff, brushed seal-grey suedes and dark hushed velvets, sleek cerise leather – perfect for cherry picking. The slipping off of a glove can make a lady tremble.

The slipping on of a shirt can make me tremble too. I devoted myself to their design. Destination: Turnbull & Asser, shirt-makers to the shirt-lifters: Liberace, Skirt Bogarde, Sir John Gielgud and me – not in order of importance, I hasten to add. It is upon the parchment of Turnbull & Asser's sacred tomes that my great legacy is recorded: The Horsley Shirt. Four button cuff. Five-inch turn back. Collar point: five inch (wide enough to fly). But it is the buttons that I will be remembered by – the covered buttons to be precise. There is something so rude about a naked button. I am the only male customer ever to have insisted upon covered fastenings for his shirt. They are essential. Though a shirt offers plenty of scope for the inessential, also, of course. Engraved silver stays, for instance. 'There's no point,' complained some dimwit, thereby reassuring me that that was precisely the point. Double cuffs are also an option – though it's mandatory that a few should be adorned with real diamante. A bit of spare adornment never did anyone any harm, which brings me to the umbrella. The paste ones are cheap at £200 a pop. Custom-made is a little more costly, but worth it when you can have ebony shafts, silver ferrules and embossed tip cups. It is so magnificently expensive that one can't bear to get it wet – which is all the more reason to invest in an array of summer parasols. They look so charming when furled if trimmed with red fluff.

Hats are the crowning glory of a dandy. Beau Brummell and Byron went to Locks. So did I – for four fedoras: fur felt, antelope velour, grosgrain band and bow (with feather mount), satin lining, roan leather – in four different colours. Few things look more ridiculous than a hat on a man who doesn't suit hats. But nothing looks more ridiculous than an ivory-white fedora on a man who doesn't suit hats. Which was why I wore one. I firmly believe that a hat should be kept on when you greet a lady – and left off for the rest of your life.

The look was almost complete. To hide my pallor and to show my disdain for public opinion, I resorted to cosmetics. It takes a real man to wear make-up. I wore it for revelation not concealment. My face was simply a document, a leaflet thrust into the hands of astonished bystanders, evidence that what I had seen was interesting.

It was done. I was an exquisite little monster, admiring myself in the mirror of my own creation. Everything about me was now phoney. Even my hair, which looked false, was real. If I had never existed, it is unlikely anyone would ever have had the nerve to invent me. Even I, who invented myself, had my doubts.

CHARLES BAUDELAIRE
on the Dandy

A profligate, hedonistic dandy, Baudelaire was a poet and groundbreaking art critic who challenged bourgeois values. This is an extract from *The Painter of Modern Life*, written in 1860, in which Baudelaire explores the idea that art, like fashion, is constructed and therefore artificial and ephemeral.

THE MAN WHO IS RICH and idle, and who, even if blase, has no other occupation than the perpetual pursuit of happiness; the man who has been brought up amid luxury and has been accustomed from his earliest days to the obedience of others — he, in short, whose solitary profession is elegance, will always and at all times possess a distinct type of physiognomy, one entirely *sui generis*. **Dandyism is a mysterious institution, no less peculiar than the duel**: it is of great antiquity, Caesar, Catiline and Alcibiades providing us with dazzling examples; and very widespread, Chateaubriand having found it in the forests and by the lakes of the New World. Dandyism, an institution beyond the laws, itself has rigorous laws which all its subjects must strictly obey, whatever their natural impetuosity and independence of character.

If I have spoken of money, this is because money is indispensable to those who make a cult of their emotions; but the dandy does not aspire to money as to something essential; this crude passion he leaves to vulgar mortals; he would be perfectly content with a limitless credit at the bank. Dandyism does not even consist, as many thoughtless people seem to believe, in an immoderate taste for the toilet and the material elegance. For the perfect dandy these things are no more than symbols of his aristocratic superiority of mind. Furthermore to his eyes, which are in love with distinction above all things, the perfection of his toilet will consist in absolute simplicity, which is the best way, in fact, of achieving the desired quality. What then is this passion, which, becoming doctrine, has produced such a school of tyrants? What this unofficial institution which has formed so haughty and exclusive a sect? It is first and foremost the burning need to create for oneself a personal originality, bounded only by the limits of the properties. It is a kind of cult of the self which can nevertheless survive the pursuit of a happiness to be found in someone else – in woman, for example; which can even survive all that goes by in the name of illusions. **It is the joy of astonishing others, and the proud satisfaction of never oneself being astonished.** A dandy may be blasé, he may even suffer; but in this case, he will smile like the Spartan boy under the fox's tooth.

———————

Dandyism is the last spark of heroism amid decadence.

ALEXANDER FURY
on Collecting

Alex is a fashion journalist, author, critic and curator. He writes about menswear for the *Financial Times* and is fashion features director for *AnOther* magazine. He has been collecting designer fashion and couture ever since he was a teenager and is a self-confessed obsessive. He says it's a mystery where his interest came from but his craving for beautiful things is unquenchable.

I GREW UP IN THE middle of the English countryside: fashion wasn't something I saw, not every day, not ever. I can still remember when I first saw – and bought – *Vogue*. It was in 1996 and I was on holiday with my family in Devon and saw it in a newsagent. It was then that I realised it did not in fact cost the same as a designer dress, something for some reason I remember I always assumed. Naomi Campbell was wearing a bikini on the cover, and it had an Obsession fragrance strip stuck inside. That smell will always take me back to then and there, to that first window into fashion. The magazine was my gateway into a world of high fashion and rarefied taste – but also more, into the universe of designers, their obsessions and loves. I knew immediately it was my home. I spent my teenage years in the local library, working my way through surprisingly well-stocked shelves, and through the history of fashion.

My mother didn't buy *Vogue*. I grew up outside Bolton, in a family that had no interest in high fashion. My mother liked clothes and enjoyed dressing up, but it was very much high street - I remember her buying what I now realise were copies of Vivienne Westwood platform shoes from Dolcis in the 1990s. As a gay child there was a lot of dancing around in her sequined cocktail dress, pretending to be Diana Ross, but I didn't dress in a particularly flamboyant way aside from that. It was more that I noticed what people wore and considered what I was going to wear. But when I discovered that there was such a thing as high fashion, that became all I wanted. I remember begging my mother to buy me a particular suit – skirt suit, I hasten to add – that I had fallen in love with for my Christmas and birthday present combined. I would say to her, 'You can wear it, but it will be mine.' Even then, there was something about the power of these objects that appealed to me.

I began to buy designer clothes when I was thirteen. I wouldn't buy diffusion lines, ever. I wanted the quality and precision of design of the piece that had been in the catwalk show and would save up my money until I could buy something small-piece in the sales. I am a snob, I always have been – but it is a snobbism based on design values, not merely for the sake of showing off a label. It's about getting the best.

I'd now say that I grew up in the golden age of British fashion. It was the late 1990s, Alexander McQueen was at Givenchy, and John Galliano at Dior. They were making fantasy gowns and spectacular pieces that really appealed to a kid's imagination. I discovered *Fashion TV* on satellite, where they covered the runway shows from Paris, New York, Milan and London. The first show I watched – the first fashion show I ever saw moving, not in a newspaper or a magazine – was McQueen, spring/summer 1996, a show called *The Hunger* after the Catherine Deneuve film. There was a corset made of PVC, sandwiching tapeworms against a woman's body. It was extreme.

My template for what makes fashion fashion was set by exposure to that period – when the clothes were extraordinary, and a show was an otherworldly, immersive experience. My ideal fashion show takes place in a tumbledown mansion with fallen chandeliers and drifts of leaves piled up, with supermodels emoting to techno music, wearing crinolines and kimonos, and fiendishly complicated bias-cut dresses. It's Galliano shows from the 1990s, basically – shows with a story, shows loaded with emotion and feeling. I fell in love with all that. I still see fashion as fantasy, escapism, a total experience that's beautiful and poetic. Fashion at this level is full of meaning and tied to narrative. When I discovered Vivienne Westwood, John Galliano, Christian Lacroix, Alexander McQueen and Azzedine Alaïa, it was like finding other people who saw the world in the same way that I did. And that meant so much to a weird kid growing up in the middle of the countryside, with his nose pressed to the glass of fashion, dreaming about Paris couture. It's so personal. I don't think of 'luxury brands'; I think of designer fashion, which is how we talked about it in the 1990s. I value a piece made by a single person, with singular vision.

When I first started buying vintage fashion, the pieces were intended to be part of my own wardrobe. I couldn't buy things simply for the pleasure of owning them – my funds just didn't run to that. That changed when I was studying Fashion History and Theory at Central Saint Martins, working on my dissertation. I was writing about a designer called Antony Price – he dressed Roxy Music in the 1970s, and his work is cult and rare, hard to find even in museums. I found two of his dresses on eBay for £10 each. That was the first time I bought something without ever intending to wear it – they were amazing, beautiful dresses, perfect objects. And they were cheap, so I just carried on collecting him. I still do.

It's never really been about what I'm wearing. I'm not that interested in clothes for myself, truth be told. I'm not stylish. I can look reasonably pulled together, but I tend to dress anonymously. My partner can look at a rail of clothes and pull out the pieces that will look great together. He's the same with cooking, whereas I can follow a recipe and wear a uniform but I'm not great at deviating from either. I suspect that, although you can learn to be more stylish, there must be an innate seed of style from which your style can develop. Mrs Prada is the most stylish woman in the world for me.

Why do I collect? Well, Wallis Simpson once said, 'The possession of beautiful things is thrilling to me.' **The clothes I collect look incredible when you see them as images but are even better when you receive them as objects. They represent extreme beauty and extreme artistry. They exceed my fantasies – the fantasies I had of these clothes when I was a kid.** That's a big thing behind my collecting.

I'm currently negotiating for a dress from the spring/summer 1994 show by John Galliano - a vast silk crinoline. That collection was called Princess Lucretia and was based on the possibly apocryphal story of Anastasia, the last Romanov princess, escaping Russia. The skirts were held out with telephone wire rather than whalebone because John said that he wanted the dresses 'to move like an echo'. There's such magic to that. I'm actually blown away that these things still exist: I assumed many were one-offs, made for shows and then subsequently lost. Every time I manage to find them, I feel a thrill. I get goosebumps. I take pieces out of their boxes and show them to people who come round to my house – it's not about bragging, 'Look what I've got.' It's more about, 'Look at this. Look at how fucking beautiful this is. Isn't this fucking great? Can you believe it?' I love that feeling.

The first piece I bought with my own money:

A pair of Vivienne Westwood jeans that I bought when I was thirteen, from the tiny Westwood shop in Manchester. They were the only thing I could afford. I wore them until they fell apart.

The one piece I'd save if my home was on fire:

A coat by Azzedine Alaïa. He and I were friends, in the last few years of his life. I loved Azzedine, and I'm happy to say he loved me. When I was in Paris, I was always invited to stay in a small apartment he owned above his shop in the Rue de Moussy and eat lunch and dinner in his kitchen. Azzedine had been an idol of mine ever since I discovered fashion, so this was totally thrilling. For me, it was like having dinner with Picasso. I still pinch myself when I think about those times with him.

One time, I had tried on a coat earlier in the day in the Alaïa store. One of the assistants must have noticed how much I loved it and spoken to Azzedine. When I arrived back at the Rue de Moussy that evening, he greeted me with, 'I've got something for you.' It was that coat, that I loved so much. But Azzedine was exacting, precise: so he fitted the coat on me, in the small *cabine* in the Alaïa store, with a smashed plate portrait of him by Julian Schnabel. His hands kneaded the fabric, moving the buttons, pinning. It was an extraordinary experience.

Azzedine was a wonderful human being - generous, kind, incredibly funny, a genius. He loved fashion, and he loved that I love fashion. That's really what we bonded over, I think. He died not long after that, so the coat is deeply sentimental for me. I would never let it go. Because I'll never let Azzedine go.

EUNICE OLUMIDE
on Vintage Sportswear

'Scotland's first Black supermodel,' but before fashion, there was athletics: she was an Olympic-level sprinter whose love of sportswear was born on the track. She's also a DJ, an actor, a gallerist, a TV presenter, an advocate for social and racial justice and an unapologetic lover of bling.

PEOPLE WILL ALWAYS NEED FUNCTIONAL fashion that you can work and travel and just generally live in. What I love about sportswear is that it delivers by being comfortable and practical, but it's also stylish. The style is shaped by the functionality, for sure, but sportswear has been worn on the streets for generations now. That transition has been propelled by youth culture and specifically by Black hip hop culture, and now it's become almost like jeans — part of the everyday wardrobe for millions of people all over the world. I'm fascinated by all that rich history, what it represents and how it plays out.

The different brands have different vibes. If you choose Adidas, that speaks to a certain historical moment and certain style values. When I was a teenage athlete, I wore Adidas. Their shoes were aerodynamic, they were all about actually *doing* sport. I wore them to run in but also when I got into skate and BMX. They were practical — much less likely to get caught in the spokes of my bike's wheels than a high top — but also a better fit with the sense of myself I wanted to project than a low-top Nike. Adidas is cool, authentic, even revolutionary; they pioneered working with early hip hop artists, for example. Nike is more straightforwardly aspirational. Mind you, Nikes are so comfortable and the brand

109

has always been brilliant at creating shoes you feel you somehow have to have. So when I jumped off my bike, I would put on a pair of Air Force or Jordans.

These days I wear a lot of sportswear for fashion, not function. I'm very concerned about sustainability and the ethics of who is making our shoes and clothes and how those people are being treated. Most of what I buy is second-hand. I love vintage US baseball shirts. I take them to a tailor and get them fitted. I also love Japanese street style. In Japan, people get their baseball shirts not just tailored but personalised, with their names. You can pick those up in thrift stores in Tokyo. Afro-Japanese style is very me! I also wear onesies by a brand called Onepiece, for my DJ gigs. They're perfect when you're touring and for performing – mad comfy and mad stylish at the same time. I've got a pinkish-green sheeny one, a camouflage one, various different colours and designs. They've become my perfect utility wear.

I also hunt down vintage Avirex jackets. **Avirex is an NYC-based menswear brand that makes jackets that combine the look of a bomber with a slightly preppy, baseball jacket feel. That stuff is hard to get hold of.** There's plenty of it new, but the old skool stuff is pretty rare . . . I go on expeditions to New York and trawl thrift shops. People are so into it. Guys come up to me in the street and they're pointing at my jacket. They're like, 'Sis, sis . . .' They can't even get their words out.

My absolute favourite is Brooklyn-based heritage brand, Walker Wear, whose clothing range was loved by nineties hip hop mega-stars like Biggy Smalls, Snoop Dogg and Tupac. When I discovered it during a US tour, I became obsessed with the designer and founder, April Walker. She created this label, turned it into a multi-million-dollar business and worked as a stylist for all those guys back then. She really contributed to the global explosion of hip hop as the defining youth culture of its time. Her brand shaped a whole style movement and yet, as a woman of colour, she's been practically written out of the story

— as Black women designers, stylists, musicians, artists so often are.

The Black tradition of hip hop and sportswear is amazing but it's also very male. Black women in popular culture don't tap into streetwear as much as men. Women music artists are consistently marketed in terms of sexuality — it's always a goddess vibe that gets pushed. There are so few Black women directors, producers, cinematographers, designers, so Black women still rarely get to represent themselves. The way we're expected to dress puts the brakes on our capacity to innovate and tells us we're not allowed to be authentic.

When Black women *do* get creative control, they really step into their style power. Look at Missy Elliot in playful tracksuits, loads of logos, bling and big hoop earrings. Or Lauryn Hill bringing together colour and tailoring, grunge and denim and streetwear and so many hats, to create a unique look. Then there's Janelle Monáe in her fantastical surreal creations or incredible menswear . . . These women are beyond creative, so talented and they have incredible and inventive style. They're next-level stylists. And yes, they're acclaimed, but there aren't many of them and they're not as big or as well-known by the public — despite multiple starring roles in film, platinum albums, awards, etc. The music industry continues to prefer Black women to be straightforwardly sexy. Which affects how Black girls and young women are allowed to see themselves.

So for me, wearing sportswear as a Black woman is subversive. It's a way to resist that hyper-sexualised style that I'm expected to fall into. I feel like I'm reclaiming my identity. When I wear sportswear I feel liberated, almost asexual, and much less visible than if I were wearing a dress. Interestingly, though, when I'm walking around Edinburgh, where I live, I get the feeling that people sometimes find a Black woman in sportswear intimidating.

The more successful I become, the more I sense a pressure to get sophisticated and classy but that's never going to be me. I love bling too much, for a start. I wear a lot of gold, up to ten chains at a time. I mostly wear it off-duty rather than when I'm working, though, or even out and about in public. I think that look is perceived as a bit cheap and a bit ostentatious at the same time. Not very British, perhaps. But I love it!

The one piece I'd save if my home was on fire:

It would have to be my baby-blue Avirex jacket.

MALCOLM MCLAREN
on Running Wild

Cultural provocateur, rock musician and manager of the Sex Pistols, the iconoclastic Malcolm McLaren (1946–2010) was a visionary who helped shape the punk movement in the UK and beyond. His words below were on display at the *Beyond the Streets, London* exhibition at the Saatchi Gallery in 2023.

AT THE AGE OF TWENTY-FIVE, I designed one of my first pieces of clothing: a bright blue lamé suit, my first rock 'n' roll suit, which I intended to wear walking the length of the King's Road. I was looking for one of those chance rendezvous that would change my life. This was 1971. I had a bag of old records that I thought I might sell and I walked. And I walked. But nothing happened. Eventually I reached the end of the King's Road, and just as I was turning around the bend known as World's End, a man popped out from what looked like a black hole among the shops.

'You,' he said. 'What are you doing here?' He had a big, black pompadour haircut and a strong Brooklyn accent.

I said that I had some records to sell.

'Why don't you come in here and sell them?'

He pointed out a dark, cavernous place, 430 King's Road . . . It was called Paradise Garage. By the time I left, my life had changed in the following respects: I had a job and a store. Patrick Casey, an art-school friend of mine, offered to join me, and the two of us set up business in the back of Paradise Garage (we called our store, appropriately enough, In the Back of Paradise Garage). We sold second-hand records and teddy-boy suits (draped jackets with velvet lapels and drainpipe trousers). And then one day the man at the front of the shop disappeared and never returned. Suddenly his shop, this hole in the wall, was ours to run too.

We changed the name to Let it Rock, and between us and my girlfriend Vivienne Westwood, we set out to make an environment where we could truthfully run wild. The shop rarely opened until eight in the evening and for no more than two hours a day. More important, we tried to sell nothing at all. Finally, we agreed that it was our intention to fail in business and to fail as flamboyantly as possible, and only if we failed in a truly fabulous fashion would we have a chance of succeeding.

It wasn't long before the store was perceived as a success – it had become an oasis at the end of the glitterdom of the King's Road – and, adhering to our founding principles, we concluded that there was only one thing to do: close it. We wanted to appear to be failing. We reopened a little later as another store, with a different name: Too Fast to Live, Too Young to Die.

In our new incarnation, we made clothes that looked like ruins – creating something new by destroying old stock. I loved making T-shirts, for example, that I would dye different colours, tread upon, trample, and generally mess up as much as possible. I wanted them to look as if they were just some old rags left underneath a car in a garage. I would adorn them with slogans: 'It's forbidden to forbid', 'Be reasonable, demand the impossible', 'Keep the dialectic open'. No one, I was convinced, would ever buy these.

I then took them and rolled them on the ground. I was very pleased with the result. **I had succeeded in taking an article of clothing that was crisp and new and white and making it into something that now suggested something wild and primitive.** This wasn't fashion as a commodity. This was fashion as an idea.

PAM HOGG
on Signature Looks

Pam is an icon of the British art and fashion scenes.
A designer, filmmaker and musician, her career has
taken her from the nightclubs of post-punk London
via supporting the Pogues, Blondie and The Raincoats
to creating costumes for the Scottish National Theatre
and performers such as Siouxsie Sioux and Lady Gaga.
Pam says she's interested in clothes, not fashion.

WHEN I WAS ABOUT FOUR, a gang of Glasgow teddy boys in their
coloured drapes and greased-back quiffs had me staring in wonder-
ment. Today, my wardrobe contains five men's drape suits, which
I've collected and customised to fit over a period of at least thirty
years. My taste in clothes is instant and lasts until it's threadbare.
I have very few clothes, so it's generally a choice of colour that
determines what I wear day to day. I tend to get dressed in a hurry
and don't leave myself much time, so sometimes I realise that my
outfit is not matching my mood and have to find something else
at top speed. But unless I'm going to an event, I don't really think
about anyone seeing me. I'm generally just heading out to cycle
to my studio and get on with work. My quiff, on and off in
numerous colours but mostly pink or canary yellow, has become
a kind of trademark look. I've been dyeing my hair and mixing
my own colour for as long as I've been collecting drape suits. I've
a very pale Scottish skin so I like the stark contrast of a red lipstick.
Lipstick, hair, footwear and sunglasses, in that order, are the most
crucial elements of a look for me, other than clothes.

I've always been a bit of an outsider. As a child I used to rake
through bags of hand-me-down clothing, recognising the jewels

115

that flamed my imagination. I was making my own clothes from the age of six, with no desire to be like anyone else or to fit in, so when 'punk' arrived I felt an immediate connection; unorthodox was in my DNA. I studied fine art and printed textiles at the Glasgow School of Art but I have no formal training in fashion design. When I got to London in the late seventies, I was more into music than anything else. I was singing in bands and spending a lot of time going to gigs and clubs. I knew I needed outfits to get past Steve Strange on the door at his club night, Blitz, but I couldn't find what I wanted to wear, so I created it.

At the Blitz I connected with all these like-minded creatures who were hellbent on dressing for pleasure while retaining their dynamic individuality. They rescued me in a way. In 1981 my friend the late Alan MacDonald sneaked me into Vivienne Westwood and Malcolm McLaren's first catwalk show: Pirates. I wore my Westwood/McLaren black spiked Seditionaries boots and couldn't believe the joy and irreverence in their clothes. Before that show I thought of fashion as dictatorial and conformist. The combination of the Blitz and Vivienne Westwood gave me a reason to apply my imagination to fashion as well as music.

There's no separation for me between designing clothes, songwriting, videos or films and performing. Everything starts with a feeling, which materialises in whatever medium it heads towards. Sometimes it's everything at once, but every medium feeds off the others. I work all the time and can work very quickly and instinctively but I also let things mull over in my imagination, returning to them every so often. I started shooting a film twenty-five years ago, for example, but had no time to edit it. Hopefully it will surface in the next year or two, along with a whole new look. I see the garments I design morph into something else over time. They are never finished. Lucinda Chambers was always requesting pieces when she was at *Vogue*. I'd never met her and didn't know who she was the first time she asked but she gave me fantastic coverage. She would send me a photo of an archive piece, asking if it was still available and I would reply, 'Well, it looks like this now!' I would have adorned it or transformed it in some way that made it very different. The fabrics I use in my designs are pieces I find, like treasures. I spot textures and colours like a magpie, immediately envisaging their purpose.

I've been designing and making catsuits for many years. They started as a way to learn to pattern cut. I would draw the lines onto my own body to understand the balance of shapes. This method gave me confidence and in turn gave confidence to the garment. Wearing a catsuit is bold. Many of the women who wanted them were initially excited but also a little afraid, until they tried them on. Then they realised that my suits give them power.

In 2014 I made a collection to honour Pussy Riot. I wasn't going to be showing that season, but three weeks before London Fashion Week I received an email from Amnesty International, asking if I'd give a nod to Pussy Riot. As I started to write my apology, I envis-aged them on their release from prison - still defiant and with so much courage. That's when I realised I was already designing a collection in my head and had the title: COURAGE. Within seconds I'd changed my response to 'Yes, of course.' For a rightful cause I'll be there in whatever capacity I can.

I've always made things to please myself and that seems to resonate. People say, 'I feel you're designing just for me.' I genuinely don't feel I have to worry about whether my work is liked or not. I give people what they don't yet know they want. I offer something new.

Style is intrinsic and can't be bought. It can be mimicked, but that impression can't be maintained for ever. I teach fashion students and I try to help them recognise the best in their own work rather than constantly looking at others and wanting to be like them. Recognising what makes you tick and brings you joy has the power to make you feel invincible.

SUSIE CAVE
on Style as a Shield

Susie Cave is the designer and co-founder of the fashion label The Vampire's Wife, which makes famously exquisite dresses. As a model, she worked closely with Vivienne Westwood for more than a decade. Her image became part of British Goth-rock legend when she was photographed wearing a long black hooded cape in Kensal Green cemetery for the cover of the Damned's 1985 album, *Phantasmagoria*.

TENSIONS ARE VERY INTERESTING IN matters of style. I love a clean simple silhouette, for example, but I also like complex Gothic drama, so these contradictions inhabit my dresses. Gothic style is perhaps the only fashion trend on Earth that deals explicitly with sorrow, darkness, mystery, spirituality, magic and even death. How strange that this most enduring of fashion statements refuses to turn away from these ideas. It says something about our preoccupations as human beings.

That said, life and style alike require an appreciation of the light as well as the shade. To maintain a sense of humour in the face of things remains paramount. I hate stuffiness and pretentiousness and I try to keep a lightness of touch around The Vampire's Wife. In an industry that seems to take itself ever more seriously, playfulness is a form of rebellion.

Really, all I'm trying to do is make beautiful things. When I worked as a model I became a student of beauty. I studied the mechanics of the exquisite; what works and what doesn't. It's architecture. By the time I left modelling, the one thing that I knew *to my core* was what looked beautiful on a woman and what didn't. I had no formal training whatsoever in dressmaking or design but when I started I knew exactly how I wanted the dresses to perform in order to enhance the natural beauty of the female form. Nothing more, really. I am embedded in my own particular vision of what I think is beautiful but my dresses seem to appeal to fellow beauty-seekers who want something unapologetically and defiantly feminine. Something unrepentantly beautiful.

I've always been inspired by folk tales. I have a beautiful book called *The Fairy Tale Tree*. I love the tales in this strange, old book; their darkness, their ferocity, their romance. **At the heart of every fairy tale there is a terrible darkness, surrounded by sweet innocence. I like this. It's in all the clothes I make, a contradiction, a sorrow.** Inspiration for my designs comes from art, music, poetry, the natural world and things I find in antique shops and junk stores. I'm very curious and try to pay attention.

Recently, for example, I wandered into an antique shop. A small ceramic figurine of a little shepherd boy tending to his sheep caught my eye. It was painted in the most gorgeous pastel colours; they were so creamy, so milky, that they were barely colours at all. That night I designed a dress that had the same milky delicacy, a very beautiful, ghost-like dress. I am very excited about it, and it may become a colour theme that runs through the next collection. I don't know. The point, I guess, is that **inspiration can come from the smallest and most softly spoken of things, as long as you remain attentive to them.**

Style can undoubtedly be a way to express yourself but it can also be a means to protect yourself. There's a counter-intuitive link between flamboyancy and reserve. I have worn some very theatrical clothes in my time and when I was a model, being photographed at all sorts of occasions was just part of my work. But I am not somebody who seeks out the limelight. I'm very shy. I am basically a hermit who spends most of her time hiding away. **Exuberant clothing, grand fashion gestures, they can be an extremely effective way of hiding.** Style as a protective shield.

I've observed the same thing with many of my friends who dress in a loud or provocative way — that deep inside they are quite awkward, reserved people.

The clothes we wear allow us to tap into mysterious forces and to communicate with others who feel as we do. For many Goths, of course, their style is not merely a fashion choice but a whole lifestyle. The thing I love about Gothic style above all else is its strange capacity to *endure*. From its origins in the post-punk scene in the early eighties to the present day, it just keeps on keeping on. I find that so moving.

The first piece I bought with my own money:

A pair of Mr America jeans, when I was fourteen years old. The factory that produced them was in Bromley High Street, which is where I lived as a teenager. I loved them because they looked the same as Fiorucci's. I bought a pair in every colour with the money I made sweeping the floor in a hair salon in Bromley. Unfortunately, I lost them somewhere along the way.

The one piece I'd save if my home was on fire:

A red velvet ball gown that the great Alessandro Michele made for me to wear to the Met Ball some years back. He was a guiding star. I miss him deeply.

BRAM STOKER
on the Vampiric

Irish author Bram Stoker's masterpiece was his legendary Gothic horror novel *Dracula*, which was published in 1897 and whose villain, Count Dracula, continues to influence representations of vampires in popular culture to this day.

I HEARD A HEAVY STEP approaching behind the great door, and saw through the chinks the gleam of a coming light. Then there was the sound of rattling chains and the clanking of massive bolts drawn back. A key was turned with the loud grating noise of long disuse, and the great door swung back.

Within, stood a tall old man, clean shaven save for a long white moustache, and clad in black from head to foot, without a single speck of colour about him anywhere. He held in his hand an antique silver lamp, in which the flame burned without a chimney or globe of any kind, throwing long quivering shadows as it flickered in the draught of the open door. The old man motioned me in with his right hand with a courtly gesture, saying in excellent English, but with a strange intonation,

'Welcome to my house! Enter freely and of your own free will!' He made no motion of stepping to meet me, but stood like a statue, as though his gesture of welcome had fixed him into stone. The instant, however, that I had stepped over the threshold, he moved impulsively forward, and holding out his hand grasped mine with a strength which made me wince, an effect which was not lessened by the fact that it seemed cold as ice, more like the hand of a dead than a living man. Again he said,

121

'Welcome to my house! Enter freely. Go safely, and leave some of the happiness you bring!' The strength of the handshake was so much akin to that which I had noticed in the driver, whose face I had not seen, that for a moment I doubted if it were not the same person to whom I was speaking. So to make sure, I said interrogatively, 'Count Dracula?'

He bowed in a courtly way as he replied, 'I am Dracula, and I bid you welcome, Mr. Harker, to my house.'

SUSIE BUBBLE
on Harajuku

Susie is a journalist and fashion influencer who began her career on her *Style Bubble* blog. Her writing has appeared everywhere from *Vogue* to *Business of Fashion* and *Pop* magazine to *London Evening Standard*. She admires an austere all-black palette but loves full-spectrum colour, as a glance at her Instagram will affirm.

STYLE HAS ALWAYS BEEN AN essential part of my attempt to understand who I am. It's a way to explore creativity, rebellion and self-expression. I spent my childhood and adolescence passing between two cultures and two countries. We were a Chinese immigrant family living in London but we often went back to Hong Kong to visit relatives. My parents were conservative, and their values were very different to those of mainstream UK society. I used clothes to navigate my unease and reconcile the tension by bringing elements of Hong Kong fashion and culture back to my schoolfriends. I enjoyed finding ways to integrate different bits into my London life.

I was searching for myself, trying to figure out my identity, as so many of us do at that point in our lives. I went to a very rigorous, academic girls' school, so dressing myself creatively was a way of rebelling against both home and school. Living in London meant I had access to amazing vintage and charity shops, and growing up in a city where people are free to do what they want with clothes was so inspiring to me. But I also had access to a lot of South-east Asian style trends, many of which started in Japan and then filtered through the region, arriving in Hong Kong where I would pounce on them.

123

I've been fascinated by Harajuku (Japanese street style) for years. We've probably all seen photos of people in those vibrant kitsch outfits now, but back in the 1990s when I first visited Tokyo, it was genuinely amazing to me. There was just nothing like it in London. The visual effect of young people dressed up in manga cosplay or in a riot of colourful baby doll cuteness can be exhilarating, but it's the creativity that really appeals to me. And the granularity. **People take their initial inspiration, which can be a relatively broad category such as rave culture or anime, and then push it through a number of sub-genres to end up with a highly specific look that revolves around massive false eyelashes and legwarmers, say.** It's an obsessive take on style and, in its earlier days, was very much a product of a pre-internet age. There are fewer factions in street style now; the looks have become more homogenous.

Harajuku remains inherently subversive, though. In Asian cultures — admittedly I'm talking in very general terms here — we're taught from a young age to stay quiet and knuckle down, work hard, respect our elders. These are patriarchal, highly conservative cultures and that can be repressive and stifling. But, of course, people will always find ways to resist those norms. Harajuku is an assertion of playfulness, the value of youth culture and the right to self-expression.

There are other qualities in South-east Asian style that I find appealing. When I was growing up, I always felt extremely awkward about my physical appearance. There was no part of me that wanted to dress 'sexy', which seemed to be how style was presented to young women in the UK. I wasn't interested in bodycon dresses. In Hong Kong and Japan, I found a different aesthetic and a different attitude, one that said, 'Yes, of course you can layer a patterned skirt over a strangely shaped trouser and wear it all with ugly shoes.' It was a different kind of beauty, more experimental and less concerned with showing off the body. That really fostered my interest in mixing prints, colours and textures.

You see that aesthetic in Rei Kawakubo's designs at Comme des Garçons and Yohji Yamamoto's work. It's more about sculptural silhouettes than feminine elegance or sex appeal.

I've ended up taking a lot from that strand of Japanese fashion and combining it with the overt playfulness of the street style. When it comes to colour, for example, I admire Yohji's very pure vibe, that austere black-on-black palette that you also see at Belgian designers like Ann Demeulemeester, but it just feels flat on me. I know that you can do so much with texture and cut and pattern within monochrome, but I enjoy colour too much to do without it. I love saturated colours, but rather than full rainbow within one outfit, I like to use different tones of one or two colours. Playfulness is a huge part of what I'm drawn to in clothes, so it's colour, and texture and fabric that appeal to me.

Recently I went to Seoul; there is an astounding creative energy on the street there, as there was in Tokyo on the 1990s. The cartoonish exaggeration of the way people style themselves is incredible. There's a hyper-real pop aesthetic, where people take elements of otaku culture (nerding out with video games and manga and anime) and wear them in everyday life. **It looks to me like a form of resistance to all the pressure those young people are under.** I read about kids throwing themselves off buildings if they got less than 100 per cent in their exams. No wonder they're looking for joyous escape routes. I kind of love these movements that grow up without the influence of high fashion and the big houses in European capitals. People are wearing clothes absolutely on their own terms and in their own cultural context.

There has never been as much fashion as there is today, when we all have access to a range of diverse creators from all over the world. This is liberating, particularly for the designer, who can find and build their own community without showing in Milan or Paris. I'm not convinced it's wholly positive, though, especially for those of us who want to wear clothes while using our imagination. Things can feel too easy. You can get this top or those Y2K flares so you too look like Bella Hadid, all at one click. **Popular style is so easily replicated, and even something as obscure as gremlin-core can be adopted and doled out by mainstream media in seconds.** We end up with less individual style.

But London is still a great place for scenes and niches, albeit in a less overt way. It's no longer as simple as the punks hanging out in Camden and the mods in Carnaby Street; it's more about a micro-scene that springs up around a specific club night. For example, I used to live in Seven Sisters and it suddenly became an enclave of fashion students because they all wanted to go to Grow. Or people convene around a specific drag scene that's popped up . . . I see a lot of make-do-and-mend style in the clubs and on the streets, kids thrifting, making their own clothes and customising. They find Miss Sixty jeans and throwaway Miss Selfridge tops on Depop and rework them so they become treasures. People are looking for individuality again, seeking out their tribe in real life and it's still true that if you want to find your tribe, you need a city.

For me, a stylish person is anyone who knows themselves well and expresses that through what they wear. They certainly don't have to be well known or have spent a lot of money. You spot them because they're moving with and responding to their clothes, living in them at ease. It doesn't matter to me what they're wearing if they've taken ownership of their style in this way.

The first piece I bought with my own money:

There was a shop called Stitch Up in Camden, where you could buy thermal vests that had been dyed in funky colours. I thought they were the coolest thing. I didn't actually have the money to buy one when I first came across the store, when I was maybe eleven or twelve, but I did go and buy a purple vest the moment I had some money. The first vintage piece I bought was a slip skirt that I wore over jeans, religiously. From a £5 rail.

The one piece I'd save if my home was on fire:

I don't play favourites with my clothes because everything I own has some weight to it . . . But perhaps, if I really had to choose . . . it would be an old Miu Miu coat in houndstooth tweed with a lace trim. I absolutely love the combination of practical and traditional with frivolous and unexpected. I wear it all the time. And it's hanging by my front door so it would be the last thing I grabbed as I ran out; much safer than charging back up the stairs to swipe a whole rail of clothes!

GRACE CODDINGTON
on the Fashionable Life

Grace Coddington is a former model and the former creative director-at-large of US *Vogue*. Tall, regal and with an unmistakable shock of flame-red hair, it's no surprise she won a *Vogue* modelling competition in 1959, marking the beginning of an unforgettable career in the fashion world. In *Grace: A Memoir*, she shares her glamorous life story from both sides of the lens.

FASHION BECAME OF EVEN GREATER significance to me at the height of the sixties, when I began regularly flying to Paris for work. I started appearing in French *Elle*, which was then enjoying a reputation as a really good fashion magazine.

Twice a year, in January and July, my photo sessions were mainly taken up with French couture, which was traditionally shot through the night. Well-heeled clients needed to view the clothes at the couturiers' salons during the day, making them entirely unavailable any earlier for photographs. Even when modelling in the wee small hours of the morning, **I was expected to show an appropriately haughty attitude.** As the inimitable American fashion oracle and editor Diana Vreeland would say, 'A little more languor in the lips.'

Clothes were sporty, zippy, sensationally short. The modern look in fashion photographs was to be either wide-eyed, hyper-energetic, and in a hysterical rush, or floppy and passive, with knees together and feet turned in like a rag doll with badly stitched legs.

Albert [Koski] and I would aim to be at Le Drugstore in the Champs Élysées on a Saturday around midnight to buy the early editions of the English Sunday newspapers. Every other night, we could be found dancing (to a twitchy form of early French pop music called yé-yé) until dawn in the fashionable club New Jimmy's, before rushing off to work the next morning. I wore extra-small children's sweaters in Shetland wool purchased at Scott Adie in London that were all the rage among the French fashion elite, and very, very tight Newman jeans (you had to lie on the floor and energetically wriggle your way into them) that were made of paper-thin cotton velvet or needlecord and came in a huge range of wonderful colours. At the time they could be bought only from one little shop in a back street off the boulevard Saint-Germain that was regularly packed with fans. I also shopped at the ELLE boutique, which was new and completely cool. *Elle* magazine photographed select outfits, then put them into their boutique for one week to stimulate demand. My penchant for wearing super-modern, very short miniskirts was much tut-tutted by the easily disapproving French, whose fashionable and what they considered far more tasteful 'mini-kilts' fell discreetly to the knee.

My idol was a French model, Nicole de Lamargé, who was very chic and also wore 'le-mini-kilt'. She was the girlfriend of photographer and *Elle* art director Peter Knapp and was known as the models' model. She was an extraordinary chameleon who could seem absolutely non-descript until she put on her make-up, and always ended up looking a dream. When it came to creating her own look, she was very sure of herself. And her personal style really typified *Elle*. It was modern, breezy and approachable, introducing a fresh, positive, and upbeat note to the pages of the magazine. Nicole was the Linda Evangelista of her day but unfortunately died young in a car accident.

I derived a completely different, far more sophisticated sense of clothes from living among the Parisiennes and working for magazines like *Elle* and French *Vogue* — which was the one we models secretly longed to appear in, since Europe's two best-known fashion photographers, Helmut Newton and Guy Bourdin, worked for it. I was also soon made aware of the way fashion dictates style and how rapidly trends can come and go. Albert had an E-Type Jag that we drove down to Saint-Tropez every weekend; or we would put it on the train. We stayed just above the port in a small *pension* called La Ponche, took our *café complet* on the narrow balcony outside our room each morning, and rode our VeloSolex (a basic kind of moped) to the most fashionable beaches, either Pampelonne or Club 55 but more often Moorea, owned by Félix, man about Saint-Tropez and the proprietor of its chicest restaurant, L'Escale, in the port.

I sunbathed in the latest Eres swimwear made from a recently developed feather-light Lycra, but I refused to go topless even though it was the fashion of the day, thanks to Brigitte Bardot and the entirely relaxed attitude of the Saint-Tropez beaches.

I was astonished by how fashion could change so fast in a few days. You would go to the South of France one weekend and denim was in. The next weekend when you returned, everything was about little English florals. I used to get so worried that I hadn't got it right. Catherine Deneuve and her sister Françoise Dorléac were the only ones I ever saw actually wearing the hard-edged space-age clothes of Courrèges and Paco Rabanne and looking completely at ease and relaxed.

PART 4

COLOUR

'I mean, black makes your life so much simpler.
Everything matches black, especially black.'

NORA EPHRON,
I Feel Bad About My Neck

'On Wednesdays we wear pink.'

KAREN SMITH,
Mean Girls

HANS CHRISTIAN ANDERSEN
on Red Shoes

Danish master of the literary fairy tale, Hans Christian Andersen's childhood experiences and vivid imagination inspired such timeless stories as *The Little Mermaid*, *The Ugly Duckling* and *The Emperor's New Clothes*. The following extract is from *The Red Shoes*, a moral tale of a young, poor girl who is condemned by an angel to: 'dance in your red shoes until you are pale and cold, and your flesh shrivels down to the skeleton'.

KAREN WAS NOW OLD ENOUGH to be confirmed; she received some new clothes, and she was also to have some new shoes. The rich shoemaker in town took the measure of her little foot in his own room, in which there stood great glass cases full of pretty shoes and white slippers. It all looked very lovely, but the old lady could not see very well and therefore did not get much pleasure out of it. Amongst the shoes stood a pair of red ones, like those which the princess had worn. How beautiful they were! The shoemaker said they had been made for a count's daughter, but that they had not fitted her.

'I suppose they are of shiny leather?' asked the old lady. 'They shine so.'

'Yes, they do shine,' said Karen. They fitted her, and were bought. But the old lady knew nothing of their being red, for she would never have allowed Karen to be confirmed in red shoes, as she was now to be.

Everybody looked at her feet, and the whole of the way from the church door to the choir it seemed to her as if even the ancient figures on the monuments, in their stiff collars and long

135

black robes, had their eyes fixed on her red shoes. It was only of these that she thought when the clergyman laid his hand upon her head and spoke of the holy baptism, of the covenant with God, and told her that she was now to be a grown-up Christian. The organ peeled solemnly, and the sweet children's voices mingled with that of their old leader; but Karen thought only of her red shoes. In the afternoon the old lady heard from everybody that Karen had worn red shoes. She said that it was a shocking thing to do, that it was very improper, and that Karen was always to go to church in future in black shoes, even if they were old.

On the following Sunday there was Communion. Karen looked first at the black shoes, then at the red ones – looked at the red ones again, and put them on.

NIKKI LILLY
on Pink Hair

Nikki is a BAFTA- and Emmy-award-winning broadcaster, author and activist. She was diagnosed with AVM
(arteriovenous malformation) when she was six years
old. This rare condition has caused significant changes
to her appearance. Nikki speaks about living with a
visible difference, fashion and style to her hundreds
of thousands of followers on social media.

I WAS DIAGNOSED WITH MY condition when I was six and I
became very sick soon afterwards. I had to stop going to school
and give up everything I'd enjoyed doing. I had been a really
active, chatty child, into gymnastics and football and dancing,
then my life changed utterly, overnight. For the next few years
I spent long periods in hospital, and even when I was at home
I was rarely well enough to go to school. I had to find new ways
to spend my time and explore the world. I needed new forms of
escapism and self-expression.

I'd always been interested in fashion and make-up, as many
little girls are, but when I found myself struggling to understand
what was happening to my body, they became crucially important.
My appearance started to change from the age of nine or so, and
I began to make videos and post them on social media to over-
come my sense of isolation and deal with my sadness and
confusion. I realised that I could use make-up and fashion as a
way to explore my identity. I was still me, but I was also mourning
the person I had been and the life I could have had. Make-up
and clothes became something to hold on to.

For a long time, my experiments with style were about my

137

insecurity and my need to fit in, or my desire to escape from the situation I found myself in. Recently, though, as I've become more confident, they are more about self-expression and shaping my future. The transformation in how I *see* myself transforms how I *feel*. And this is true for all of us. If you can shift how you feel about yourself, you can shift how other people see you.

I don't look normal, and living in a world where we're constantly being told how we're supposed to look is hard on all of us. But no two people are the same, and style is a celebration of difference. Your unique style reflects whatever it is that makes you feel great. There are no wrongs or rights, it's way too personal for that. Although the fashion and beauty industries definitely contribute to the messages about how we 'should' look, they're also good at celebrating difference and uniqueness. I feel I can be myself in this space.

For most teenagers, music and clothes are crucial. What we choose is the basis of who we are. We have to experiment, and although I cringe when I look back at some of what I wore, I know that those clothes were all part of the journey. These days I only wear things that speak to me, that I have a vision for, that I love. It's much more curated. I'm learning who I am and having a lot of fun.

My hair has been a crucial part of that. I've had pink hair since 2018. I was obsessed with the colour rose gold and had been badgering my mum to let me dye my hair that shade. She resisted because my sister hadn't been allowed to dye hers until she was fourteen, and I was still only thirteen. But later that year, I became really unwell. I had two catastrophic bleeds and it was touch and go whether I would pull through. After one operation I was in a coma for eight days. Mum sat by my bedside, talking to me even though I couldn't respond, and one of the things she said was, 'If you wake up, you can dye your hair pink.' So the moment I left hospital, Mum dyed my hair. I don't feel like myself without it now.

I tend to wear streetwear, especially thrifted, for everyday and then go all out girly fantastical for events and parties. I love thrifting so much, it's my favourite thing. I spend a lot of time on eBay and Depop, and 99 per cent of my wardrobe is second-hand. I love the fact that these pieces have history and tell a story. It's so much more personal. Lately I've been borrowing my mum's old clothes from the nineties. She wore miniskirts with Doc Martens and colourful tights and she kept many of them. She's been a huge influence, both in terms of style and life more generally.

When I started being invited to attend red carpet events, it did feel like a dream. The process of planning and then wearing an outfit for an event like that is so much fun for someone who's always loved dressing up. **In 2021, not long out of hospital, I wore a yellow strapless dress and my new pink hair to the BFAs.** I'd never worn yellow before but a stylist suggested it and I absolutely loved it. My other favourite red carpet dress is probably the vintage sage-green Versace piece I wore to the premiere of *Game of Thrones: House of Dragons*. I wanted something that felt almost mythical, and that dress, which had been worn by Beyoncé and Christina Aguilera before me, was definitely that. It made me feel beautiful.

I had no idea when I started uploading my videos to YouTube that I would have a career as a broadcaster and end up on the red carpet at the 2019 BAFTAs ceremony, heading to collect my award. I have been the change I wanted to see, because when I was a child there was nobody in the public eye or in the media who had a story similar to mine. Now, I sit front row at fashion shows; I walked in the Oxfam show at London Fashion Week in 2022, and that makes me so happy because I feel I'm helping to make a difference. It's almost a form of activism. I'm not holding a placard; I'm simply showing up and demonstrating how far we've come and how much further we have to go.

I have taken an active decision to face the world rather than

hide away. It wasn't an overnight thing; it was a process and even now it's not easy. People do stare at me on the train and in the street and that still makes me uncomfortable, but I've tried to change the terms of why people look at me. Both my broadcasting work and my style choices reflect my decision to be more visible, not less. I appear on my own terms now. Fashion, hair, make-up: they all feel like armour. When I started, I was doing it for myself. Now I'm doing it for everyone who has a disability, who looks or feels different from mainstream society's views of what people are supposed to look like.

The first piece I bought with my own money:

A pair of Nike Dunk trainers. I remember worrying that they cost too much money but I loved them so much. I wore them to school as a way to add some fun to the uniform!

The one piece I'd save if my home was on fire:

A sequined Blumarine miniskirt with an embroidered waistband I found on Depop. I spent a lot of money on it but when I wore it on a recent trip to New York, I knew it was worth it.

MAYA ANGELOU
on Lavender Taffeta

Maya Angelou was a renowned American poet, memoirist and civil rights activist. Born in 1928 in St Louis, Missouri, her early life was marked by extreme poverty, racism and violence. Her resilience in the face of adversity and dedication to the pursuit of equality led to her becoming one of the most revered figures in history. *I Know Why the Caged Bird Sings* is the first volume of her remarkable autobiography.

THE DRESS I WORE WAS lavender taffeta, and each time I breathed it rustled, and now that I was sucking in air to breathe out shame it sounded like crepe paper on the back of hearses.

As I'd watched Momma put ruffles on the hem and cute little tucks around the waist, **I knew that once I put it on I'd look like a movie star.** (It was silk and that made up for the awful color.) I was going to look like one of the sweet little white girls who were everybody's dream of what was right with the world. Hanging softly over the black Singer sewing machine, it looked like magic, and when people saw me wearing it they were going to run up to me and say, 'Marguerite [sometimes it was "dear Marguerite"], forgive us, please, we didn't know who you were,' and I would answer generously, 'No, you couldn't have known. Of course I forgive you.'

IB KAMARA
on Telling Stories

Ib Kamara is a multi-hyphenate creative. He is currently Editor-in-Chief of *Dazed & Confused*, and Art and Image Director at Off-White™. He also creates music, videos, films and furniture. He was born and grew up in Sierra Leone and came to London, via Ghana, with his family at the age of sixteen. He draws on his West African heritage as well as his Central Saint Martins training to create a singular and powerful style that has captivated the fashion world.

I GREW UP IN A small, poor community where people took fashion very seriously. My dad and I would visit the tailors to get my clothes made – school uniform, clothes for church and special occasions like Eid and Christmas. The whole family went. It wasn't unusual in my family and our community to spend what little money we had on bespoke outfits. There were so many tailors, seamstresses and really skilled handcrafters. I remember selecting basic designs, choosing the shapes, textures and colour of the fabric and then getting measured. I loved it.

Colour is really important to me. I enjoy it and I really miss it when it's not there. The first time I visited India, I really felt bombarded by colour in a good way – it's a brilliant assault on your senses – and it was one of the things I first noticed when I got back to London; everyone seemed to be wearing dark colours on the Underground. I am generally a 'more is more' person **and I'm always aiming to tell stories through colour, fabric, detail, texture. I'm not scared of 'mess'.** When I'm designing, styling and ideating in general, I embrace disorder and then go back and edit once I've figured out the full picture of what it is I want to say. It's important to edit for impact and coherence, of course, but being scared that things will get messy can stop you from achieving something new, something that pushes boundaries.

That's what I love about fashion — it's a truly global way that everyone is connected, but style is still very specific. All over the world, people express themselves through what they choose to wear, but it looks different in New York and Lagos. In the cities of West Africa there's a lot of what people refer to as 'cheap Western clothing' but there is also a rich heritage of traditional clothing — church clothing, party clothing . . . — and when you mix it all together you get a new take on style. I think the kids in West Africa are currently living through the kind of social revolution that the West experienced in the 1960s and 1970s. People who grew up in 'the West' since the 1980s and 1990s are used to restyling ideas they've inherited from their parents' and grandparents' generations, whereas in Africa, the kids are living that sense of revolutionary exploration and disruption of social norms for the first time, for themselves. They're creating their own sub-cultures. The music is exciting, the culture, art and film scenes are vibrant and the fashion is inspiring. There is so much pride across Africa. There's a confidence among young African people and West Africa is really leading the way. I would say that eight years ago the style capital was Johannesburg. Now it's Lagos or Dakar. And, of course, there's so much cross fertil-isation of ideas via the internet, so global styles can feed one another.

I was able to study at Central Saint Martins and got to learn from and meet some of the most talented people with radical and free-thinking minds who have gone on to work in fashion, adver-tising, film, the gaming industry, so many areas. It was an education in distinctively London and UK-derived elements of style. I've been influenced by people like Simon Foxton, Barry

Kamen, Judy Blame. Those great creatives had a very punk aesthetic. I really respond to their philosophy of using found objects from lots of different contexts and reinventing them according to their own unique take on the world. I love to combine things in unexpected ways, take something from what a Sierra Leonean refugee is wearing, a Western cowboy and a nod to traditional Britishness. My work is about investigating and pushing things, twisting them to create something totally personal.

I don't consider myself an outsider, more a person who's both in and out of various groups. Barry was my mentor, and almost became a second father-figure in the end. He taught me that it was fine to have an outsider's perspective, and that you could still have a more general point of view as well. I think it's possible to operate within the system and thrive, though of course you do run the risk of ending up producing work that you think the system wants. Or needs.

Style matters because it is a representation of where you come from. Fashion is an industry based around products and brands, ultimately, but style goes beyond clothing, bags or shoes. It's lived experience. It's a feeling. It's what your grandmother wore and how she wore it. It's details and gestures. The sexy way Carine Roitfeld puts her hand in her jacket pocket when she walks: that's style. How you walk in your denim: that's style. Clothing projects what you feel and who you are, which comes from every one of your life experiences.

I feel like I dress like a teenager; I just throw a lot of things on. I love the mess of it, though I clean it up before I leave the house. I never decide what I want to wear in advance and I like to mix things up: different colours, different lengths and layers. I will wear a colourful second-skin layer, perhaps, and then put a cardigan or a cropped top over it. Or I might wear shorts with a big jacket, add a hat or a cap, beads in my hair. There's always a lot going on, but I get it and my friends get it! Style is about fun, friends, having a good time.

My work is seen as political, but I didn't set out to be an activist, it's just part of my thinking. I grew up witnessing a war in Sierra Leone. My family had to leave our village and move to safety. We had to keep running. I saw guns and violence and death. I'm not afraid to talk about it; in fact, I'm happy to talk about both the suffering and the beauty I've seen. I'm trying to contribute to a conversation with my work, and to highlight that there are so many experiences that deserve to be talked about. I like to be direct and arresting.

The first piece I bought with my own money:

When I enrolled in college in London I got a small grant, £30 a week. That was the first time I'd really ever had any money of my own. I remember going to Oxford Street with a friend. We bought as many different tops and trousers and caps as we could. The high street stores were heaven but as soon as I could I started buying vintage. I normally only buy vintage now.

The one piece I'd save if my home was on fire:

I'd be fine with letting all my clothes burn. I'd just make something new. I embrace the future. I'm always looking for what's hot, for exciting minds. That makes me want to do more, create more.

BEAU BRUMMELL
on Composition

Though he died poor and mad in France, for a time Beau Brummell was a friend of the Prince Regent, the future King George IV, and was regarded as *the* authority on men's fashion in the Regency period. This is an extract from the nattily titled, *Male and Female Costume: Grecian and Roman Costume, British Costume from the Roman Invasion Until 1822, and the Principles of Costume Applied to the Improved Dress of the Present Day*.

IN THE COMPOSITION OF COLOURS for dress, there ought to be one predominating colour to which the rest should be subordinate.

To the predominating colour the subordinate ones should bear a relation, similar to that between the fundamental or the keynote [in music] and the series of sounds constituting a musical composition. And as, in a piece of music, there is a relation between the successive sounds or notes, so in dress the subordinate colours should be in harmony with each other. The power of perceiving this relation of colours constitutes the faculty called taste in colouring.

As painters —
Permit not two conspicuous lights to shine
With rival radiance in the same design

so in dress, one half of the body should never be distinguished by one colour, and the other by another. Whatever divides the attention, diminishes the beauty of the object; and though each part, taken separately, may appear beautiful, yet as a whole the effect is destroyed. Were a particular limb differently coloured, the effect would be ridiculous. It is in this way . . . that moun-tebanks are dressed, and it never fails to produce the effect that is intended by it, to excite the mirth and ridicule of the common people.

The variety of colours which may be introduced in dress depends on the expression of the predominating colour. Delicate colours require to be supported and enlivened, and, therefore, are best relieved by contrasts; but the contrast should not be so strong as to equal the colour it is intended to relieve, for it then becomes opposition, which should always be avoided. Contrast, skilfully managed, gives force and lustre to the colour relieved, while opposition destroys its effect.

In the composition of the subordinate colours, there is a maxim of Du Fresnoy's which applies as well to the arrangement of colours in dress as in painting:

Forbid two hostile colours close to meet

And win with middle tints their union sweet.

The choice of the predominating colour will be indicated by the situation, the age, the form and the complexion of the wearer.

LUKE EDWARD HALL
on Complementing and Contrasting

Luke has designed everything from cushion covers to a hotel, and has collaborated with brands such as Lanvin, Burberry and GANT, deploying his distinctive, whimsical and nostalgic style. He is also an artist and writes a regular column on stylish living for the *Financial Times*. Whether it's a vase or a restaurant, all his projects are fuelled by a sense of playfulness and romance.

IT'S HARD FOR ME TO analyse why I love bold, vibrant, complementary and contrasting colours as much as I do. Colour and pattern are very natural ways of expressing myself. I enjoy them hugely. Colour has so much power to make us feel things. It hacks our emotions. When I come home to our flat in London, which is like a little jewel box filled with a dizzying mix of colour and pattern, it immediately lifts me up. Certain colour palettes have an almost magical ability to induce joy and optimism, and that's what my work is all about. I like to celebrate beauty and romance, the pleasure of an uplifting aesthetic experience. Colour is one of the main conduits by which I can do that.

I studied fashion at Central Saint Martins and thought I was going to design menswear, but after I graduated I got a job with an interior designer. I've always had a fondness for set design, theatre and costume as well as fashion and interiors. To style a space or a room or oneself is all part of the same story. **I get dressed the same way I put a room together: it's about finding interesting colour combinations and having fun with juxtaposing textures and patterns and periods.** My style is rooted in eclecticism, in that joyful mixing of objects from different times and places.

Perhaps that's one of the reasons that I focus so much on colour and pattern. When your style is maximalist or eclectic, it becomes especially important to find ways to make the room or the outfit feel cohesive and considered. There is always a risk of eclecticism toppling into chaos but if the colour palette and patterns have been carefully considered, they can help keep a cohesive thread running through the space. It is hard to find that perfect tension, so that a look is unpredictable but singular; experimental but still coherent. It's also hard to explain how to do it, or quantify what constitutes success. We can only figure it out through trial and error, trying to hone our instincts and our eye as we go. There is a certain amount of practice and effort required but the reward is to end up with a look that feels true to you, that taps into your interests and evokes the emotions you want to feel, the atmosphere you want to create. My golden rule for decorating is to do what you like, not what anyone else tells you is the right or tasteful choice. I think the best interiors, like the best outfits, are deeply personal.

I'm enthralled by certain historical eras, especially the inter-war period. One of my biggest influences and inspirations is Cecil Beaton, the polymath genius whose work defined glamour and elegance from the 1920s to the 1960s. He was a fashion photographer under contract to *Vogue* for thirty years, a great portrait photographer of celebrities and royalty, a three times Oscar-winning costume and set designer for theatre and film. He designed gardens, interiors and house parties for his vast circle of famous friends. His life was dedicated to the creation and recording of beauty, with romanticism, wit and elegance as his guiding principles. I've always been fascinated by people who work across a broad range of media and Beaton was a total artist. Sometimes I wish I could have met him, though he had a reputation for being rather malicious — I'm not sure how friendly he would have been!

Beaton, along with figures like the portrait painter and muralist Rex Whistler, and Oliver Messel, the stage and interior designer, epitomise that inter-war period of theatrical glamour and romance. When I look at designs from that time, they seem electric with creativity overlaid with the poignant knowledge that it was all about to be extinguished by the Second World War. I've also found a lot of inspiration in the artists of the Bloomsbury Group.

The 1960s and 1970s were a time of great optimism and creative exploration that I return to over and over for inspiration. I love David Hockney's paintings for his colour combinations that captured and defined the positivity of the era. He's a personal style inspiration, as well. He always looks slightly dishevelled, as if he's been having fun and not taking life too seriously. He does that classic English thing of wearing crisp tailoring or a classic trench coat and disrupting it with a pair of Crocs or lime-green socks. And of course the round glasses are iconic.

I also love the fresh colours and the playful elegance of designers such as Ossie Clark and Celia Birtwell. If ever I want to immerse myself in that magical optimistic 1960s and 1970s period, I turn to photographer Peter Schlesinger's work, especially his book of collected photographs, *A Chequered Past*.

I'm inspired by the romance of history and the magic of theatre. I love buying vintage clothes, antique furniture and general junk. Old pieces have character and bring something unexpected to an overall look, whether it's a room or an outfit. I love the visual trickery of *trompe l'oeil* and collect theatre costumes and props, some of which make their way into my interior schemes. I enjoy wearing the costumes I buy (the ones I can actually fit into) at parties, but many pieces I keep simply for inspiration. I buy a lot from a dealer who specialises in 1930s French theatre costume. They're just such exquisite and romantic objects. I also have a very large collection of patterned vintage knitwear.

I love to travel, especially in the cities of Europe, and I love a grand old hotel – faded but still magical. I've designed interiors for hotels and restaurants in France and Switzerland. This part of my job is interesting because I need to convey a sense of the specific location, but of course we live in a globalised world now, where elements and inspirations come from all over. I am currently designing a Peruvian restaurant in St Moritz which needs to reference both destinations, whilst at the same time incorporating my (naturally eclectic) style.

Wherever I travel, the first thing I do is locate good places to eat, bookshops, vintage clothing and junk shops, and museums. These are the spaces that allow me to tap into a sense of place, through its food, its clothes, its objects, its past and its culture. It's fun to look back to a place's history and to try to create work that is inspired by it, but still contemporary in feeling.

For me, a person is stylish when they have their own point of view and they're confident in their self-knowledge and expression. I don't necessarily need to like a person's sense of style to admire it. Minimalism, for example, is not my aesthetic at all, either in clothes or interiors, but if I see a minimalist house that's been put together by somebody who really means it, who lives and breathes it, and with an exquisite eye, I can find it amazing. Style is doing what you love, with total conviction. That's always cool.

The first piece I bought with my own money:

I was quite the goth in my early teens, which seems kind of unlikely now, given the place of colour in my style philosophy. I grew up in Basingstoke and, like many teens in suburbia, I was looking for ways to experiment with style. I used to go and spend my pocket money at a shop called Area 51, which I adored. By the time I was about sixteen, colour had taken over. I started making a fanzine about fashion and music, which I called *Cake*.

I invited my friends to contribute. It was all very DIY, full of collage. I've barely worn black since.

The one piece I'd save if my home was on fire:

Perhaps my wedding suit? Though, actually, I could make it again. So it would have to be something old and irreplaceable. It would probably be a piece of art — hard to choose, but my favourite piece I own is a drawing by the American artist Larry Stanton, who very sadly died in his thirties in 1984. It's a poignant piece.

F. SCOTT FITZGERALD
on Clothes That Make You Cry

In his most-celebrated novel *The Great Gatsby*, F. Scott Fitzgerald exquisitely captures the hedonistic essence of the Jazz Age and roaring twenties America through flapper dresses, tailored suits, lavish ballgowns and ostentatious accessories. When the story's heroine, Daisy Buchanan, witnesses enigmatic millionaire Jay Gatsby's shirt collection, she is moved to tears.

RECOVERING HIMSELF IN A MINUTE he opened for us two hulking patent cabinets which held his massed suits and dressing-gowns and ties, and his shirts, piled like bricks in stacks a dozen high.

'I've got a man in England who buys me clothes. He sends over a selection of things at the beginning of each season, spring and fall.'

He took out a pile of shirts and began throwing them, one by one, before us, shirts of sheer linen and thick silk and fine flannel, which lost their folds as they fell and covered the table in many colored disarray. While we admired he brought more and the soft rich heap mounted higher – **shirts with stripes and scrolls and plaids in coral and apple-green and lavender and faint orange, with monograms of Indian blue.** Suddenly, with a strained sound, Daisy bent her head into the shirts and began to cry stormily.

'They're such beautiful shirts,' she sobbed, her voice muffled in the thick folds. 'It makes me sad because I've never seen such – such beautiful shirts before.'

153

LUCINDA CHAMBERS
on the Language of Colour

Lucinda is a designer and stylist. She was fashion director at *Vogue* for twenty-five years, a consultant with Prada and Marni and is the co-founder of her luxury fashion label, Colville, and stylish shopping site, Collagerie. Lucinda has lived in the same house in Shepherd's Bush for thirty years, decorating it in a joyful mix of colour, print, art and sentimental pieces. She still visits Portobello Market every Friday morning.

I HAVE LOVED COLOUR EVER since I was a child. I think I got it from my mother. By the time I was eighteen, we had moved eighteen times. My mother did up flats and houses, decorating them in different styles. We didn't move off page fifty-eight of the A-Z, so it was all within walking distance of the Brompton Oratory, where she was never off her knees, and Harrods, where we would go to look at clothes. We couldn't afford anything but she would take us to pick out something we liked, try it on, measure up with the tape measure she always had in her pocket and then she'd buy the fabric, we'd go back home, and she would make all the clothes we'd tried on.

That was my mother all over. She was endlessly creative, a craftswoman. She would teach herself to build a drystone wall or create a rose garden if she felt that was what her project required. Her mantra was, 'Just try it out.' She used to say this about everything from boyfriends to jobs to styles. She was totally unafraid of change. I've never been nervous about changing styles or experimenting with colours. I once painted a bathroom electric blue; hated it, painted it over.

I've found that colours talk to one another. Whenever I'm putting collections or houses or clothes together, the colours either say hello or they walk away from one another. **There is definitely a language of colour, which can be expressed in a loud chatter or a soft muted conversation.**

Colour inspiration can come from anywhere. **I steal colours, and I find them in unlikely places,** like a hospital ward or a tile I bought at a car boot sale. I spot a particular leaf on the pavement, a belt on a market stall. You just have to keep your eyes open to discover groupings of colour in the most unexpected and everyday places. Sometimes, you have to sit on a particular combination for years before you find the moment to deploy it.

I don't think there's much distinction between clothes and interiors when it comes to colour, or style in general. Not for me, at least. When I worked at *Vogue*, my primary interest was in storytelling and what I loved most was being on a set, planning a shoot: its characters and story. My work as fashion director always started with a character. Even if the brief was, *Do a coat story*, the first thing I thought about was, *Who's the character in the coat?* So perhaps it would be a woman who's thinking about breaking up with her husband; she's a recluse, holed up in a modern house on an island in Sweden, sitting on a sofa, trying to work out whether to leave him or not . . . and, incidentally, she's wearing a coat. Then I would brief the model about her character. It was all about the setting and the mood. Clothes helped me to tell a story, but they weren't my starting point. It's the same with interiors. When I'm doing a room in my house, for example, I think about it as a set. What activities will people be doing in that space? What sort of mood will they be in?

Mood is so important. The hallway to our house was painted a very vibrant fleshy pink for years. I added a stripey carpet and the walls were full of stuff. I loved it until, one night when I was getting home late from work, I opened the door and just thought, *No*. It was suddenly wrong for me. It felt as if I was coming into the home of a mad old lady. I knew instantly that what I needed instead was to feel calm. I wanted cool earthy tones that would make me feel peaceful. **I thought of it as the colours of a German urinal. I'm not quite sure why.** I just had a sense that I wanted grey, blue, brown, and a very thin black line dividing the brown below from the grey and blue above. It's been ten years now and I still find that combination grounding and soothing.

I don't have favourite colours or stock combinations, either for walls or clothes, though I do wear a lot of navy, cream and khaki. I love neutrals, and I love having a sort of uniform for those days when you just don't want to think about what you're wearing too much. I tend to have uniform days and then much more colourful days, when I feel the mood and really want to go for it.

I never underestimate how nervous some people are with colour but I think that if you can just find the base colour that suits you, then you can start to experiment. So, in my case, that colour is khaki because I have muddy green eyes. **If you're not sure what suits you, think about the last time a friend paid you a compliment.** Your base colour might be cream, black, navy, pink . . . Whatever it is, you can then layer other colours over it, in different quantities. Perhaps you add navy to cream and then a pair of green earrings. Even if you're nervous, you can still creep up on colour.

I celebrate when I see a stylish person out and about, on the Tube. Often it's an older woman or a young kid, and their enjoyment of fashion is obvious. Recently I was on my way to the Barbican when I saw a woman in her seventies. She looked amazing, with her lipstick and a fabulous necklace and a sparkly blue boot and coloured hair. . . Blue was her colour and she'd gone for it; she was enjoying herself so much. Or look at Iris Apfel, aged ninety; you couldn't squeeze another bangle on her arm. She's having the best time. Or kids who have a new look every time I see them, like my godchildren. Fabulous; they're all just trying things out.

You can learn style; you don't have to be born with it, but it takes quite a lot of effort, and you will fail a lot. That's very important: don't be afraid of failing. Also, don't underestimate how important it is to be comfortable. If you can't walk in the heels, if you can't move around, if your trousers are too tight, you're never going to look stylish. Above all, have fun and be curious about life and other people.

The first piece I bought with my own money:

When I was growing up, I bought a lot of my clothes from jumble sales; I still love thrifting, car boot sales and markets. The first big purchase was a Yohji Yamamoto jacket. I bought it for £400, which is still a lot now but was a fortune for me then. I don't have it any more. I prefer to sell my clothes on, partly to raise money for charity, partly because I love to see my clothes have a second life with somebody else. I once sold a Prada skirt for £40 to a woman who told me she'd loved that particular Prada collection and was so delighted to finally be able to wear it.

The one piece I'd save if my home was on fire:

I don't have a strong emotional attachment to clothes but I would definitely save my mother's ring. It was her signature piece; she wore it every day of her life. And now, so do I.

FLORENCE GIVEN
on Loving Leopard Print

Florence is the bestselling author of *Women Don't Owe You Pretty* and *Girl Crush*. She's also an illustrator, advocate for women's and queer rights and the host of the hit podcast *Exactly*. A style obsessive, she curates her outfits, her home and her world with a joyful maximalist vibe.

I GREW UP IN PLYMOUTH in a household where dressing up, making clothes and drawing were all encouraged. I used to borrow my grandmother's costume jewellery and evening gloves to perform shows for my family. When I was ten I customised a dress to wear for my primary school prom with a huge bow I'd made out of spotty fabric. I was obsessed with Lady Gaga. I remember watching her 'Paparazzi' video, just crying my eyes out. **I recreated the cigarette sunglasses with white and brown paper stuck on a pair of Primark shades and the diamanté ones from the *Fame* album cover.** She was my style pinup.

Colour and exuberance and exploration through style always came naturally to me so it was only later that I realised how much of it had flowed from my mum, her cousin and my mum's friend. They had a very 1970s take on Art Deco glamour, which has really influenced my own choices. Lots of fringed lampshades and Biba prints on the walls, leopard print sofas and brightly coloured cushions with tasselling everywhere.

I absolutely inherited my love of leopard print from Mum. I have two velvet leopard print sofas in my home now, which are so warm and luxurious. Leopard is the epitome of luxury for me, but it has to be the good kind: not just splodges of black on brown. I like it to have a depth of colour and variety within the print. It's a neutral, a baseline, and you can style it with anything. Whenever I see it or wear it, I just feel so delicious. It's rock and roll, it's glamour and comfort and fun. Everything all at once.

I'll always be a seventies gal. That look is just hot! I love the feminine style but I'm also really drawn to its queer energy. Joan Jett in sharp suits, for example. Or Penny Lane in *Almost Famous* – though the aesthetic not the lifestyle. I love the way the fashion of that era feels frankly sexual, but the vibe isn't about dressing for men. It's more female-centric. It's sex appeal without doing what men want you to do.

I use style as a means of self-expression and a way to go beyond my comfort zone. I want to convey the way I see the world and myself with everything I do, whether it's my writing, my visual art or my clothes. I have a magpie eye and I constantly notice detail about colour, pattern and form. I'm always taking in ideas and inspiration, working on them and then putting something back out there. Whether it's an outfit or a piece of art, projecting my inner world is like the completion of a cycle. There's no more euphoric feeling.

Style and identity are so entwined. So is the way you perceive yourself and others perceive you. Making deliberate choices about how you present yourself means you get to tell the world a little bit about yourself without even opening your mouth. That can be powerful. I started to really get this when I came out as bisexual. By the time I was sixteen, I'd told my friends and family but I didn't come out online until a little later, when I was about nineteen. My style at the time was very feminine and a lot of people who followed me were really surprised. They perceived me as straight because of the way I dressed. That didn't add up for me. I felt bisexual but I wasn't being perceived that way. It wasn't about suddenly wanting to look gay; it was more about dressing the full range of who I am, but it also made me start asking myself questions – did I actually *like* dressing that way or was it just my idea of how a woman *should* look and behave?

My hair has been a bit of a case in point. I used to have very long blonde hair down to my bum and that became part of my identity. Once my career took off, I found my online audience loved it, which was kind of a beautiful thing but then began to feel a bit oppressive. This aspect of myself that I had loved was no longer simple. So almost as an act of rebellion, I cut it all off and had a shaggy shoulder-length cut for a while. That was very freeing. The same cycle happened again with my Farah Fawcett flicky style, which I absolutely love but ended up becoming almost a trademark, to the point that I started to feel I was dressed as a character rather than myself. I was wearing my hair in this ultimate sexy feminine seventies style with a tailored trouser suit and a pointy boot or some platforms, feeling great, but it coincided with a time when I was doing a lot of promotion for my book and after a while it was almost like being in drag. So I lost the Farah curls and now my hair is bright pink. I'm growing it long again so that I can wear it in plaits, with lots of ribbons woven through.

It's become a habit for me, to be constantly thinking about style and the visual realm. I put a lot of effort into beautifying my environment because it improves the quality of my life. It's like taking life off the default setting and making it custom. Anybody can do it; it just takes intention.

The one piece I'd save if my home was on fire:

My mum gave me a leopard print bucket hat she wore back in the 1990s. I don't wear it that much any more but I still love it; and if I ever have a daughter, I'll be passing it on to her.

SYLVIA PLATH
on Her Little Black Dress

One of the most celebrated and controversial poets of the twentieth century, Sylvia Plath's legacy is profound and far-reaching. Her intensely personal work continues to captivate readers and inspire conversations about mental health, feminism and the search for one's true self. The extract below is from her semi-autobiographical novel *The Bell Jar*, which was published shortly before she tragically took her own life in 1963.

I WORE A BLACK SHANTUNG sheath that cost me forty dollars. It was part of a buying spree I had with some of my scholarship money when I heard I was one of the lucky ones going to New York. The dress was cut so queerly I couldn't wear any sort of bra under it, but that didn't matter much as I was skinny as a boy and barely rippled, and **I liked feeling almost naked on the hot summer nights.**

OLIVIA SINGER
on Only Black

Olivia is the Global Editorial Director at *i-D* magazine and has previously worked at British *Vogue* as Fashion News Director and *AnOther* magazine as Fashion Features Director. The owner of an exquisite all-black wardrobe of high fashion, her style is glamorous with an edge.

I DIDN'T EXPECT TO END up working in the fashion industry. I wasn't one of those teenagers who devoured magazines and made all my own clothes. I grew up in London during the indie years of the early noughties, going to gigs and clubs. My style was vaguely alternative but what I wore wasn't the defining element of how I thought about myself: me and my friends sort of shared our wardrobes, and just kept communal piles of clothes we liked on each other's floors.

After I went to university, I was fairly unmoored and spent some time in Paris trying to figure out what to do next. I worked in a kitchen, and as part of a feminist collective, and then I got a job in a vintage clothes shop. That's when my interest in fashion became more prominent – we used to buy whole wardrobes after people died. I remember one woman who had the most incredible style. When we went through her clothes, we could trace the evolution of her taste and the changes in her body; they became her biography. She had been a model in the 1920s, wearing dresses and tiny tab shorts, then a travel journalist who brought back ponchos and kaftans from South America. There were Chanel suits from her later years spent as a Parisian lady. It's the sense of self that is expressed through clothes that interests me most. I often feel that's inextricably linked to the body.

In my early twenties, after moving back to London, I snuck into a Meadham Kirchhoff show with a friend, and suddenly everything changed. I realised how fashion designers could create a sense of community and invite you into their world. The show was Riot grrrl feminism incarnate; it didn't denigrate the aesthetics of femininity or see it at odds with strength and rebellion. It had music, politics and aesthetics all in one place, and felt far more instinctively reso-nant than the academic feminism I was tangled up in. The designers and brands I love now – Comme des Garçons, Rick Owens, Martine Rose – all do a similar thing. They create their own immersive worlds and, through that, attract a tribal, cultish following. I've spent months on end thinking about how Rei Kawakubo or Miuccia Prada have made me feel at a fashion show, and then the clothes I buy from those collections become like totems of that consideration.

I wear black, almost exclusively. My hair is black and cut into a short bob with a heavy fringe. I like to wear dark glasses, and I like to wear my dresses tight. I suppose the look is a bit gothy, a bit dramatic. Quite sexy. Sticking to a singular aesthetic wasn't necessarily a conscious decision; partly, it's about practicality. **Black always matches, and it doesn't get dirty, which is useful because I'm a little dishevelled and I smoke all the time. Black also enables you to both fade into the background and stand out when you want to.** The absence of colour also means there are fewer distractions from the fundamentals of the piece. When you wear black, you have to pay attention to fit and fabric, which are the elements of clothes that I find most interesting.

Also, I've found that black allows me to feel more comfortable in my body. I'm short and have hips, and that means that I don't really have the body required for certain sorts of fashion favourites. Beauty standards are still so insane and, like many women, I feel their impact. I am friends with some women who are celebrated as the world's most beautiful: women who appear on magazine covers and open and close fashion shows. They are routinely told that they're not thin or beautiful enough, and agonise over their appearance, which proves the point that nobody is ever going to be 'good enough' by these bizarre, arbitrary definitions. It's why I love designers who consider the wearer in their process of creation and are expanding notions of beauty and inclusion. So much of fashion is about image-making, which can be absolutely wonderful, but it's an entirely different skillset to create clothes that make women feel powerful.

I'm not a casual dresser. I don't do denim. I have a couple of pairs of trainers that I might wear if I'm travelling but otherwise, I wear tight skirts and dresses with very high heels pretty much every day. That's how I feel comfortable. I've always dressed sexy, in bodycon and heels. I remember being on one Reclaim the Night march around twenty years ago, and an older feminist told me that I was bringing down the movement because of what I was wearing. I was helping to organise the march – a march which was about liberation.

Clothing is powerful, and women are subject to a million different opinions and expectations about how we present ourselves, but I resent the idea that any of us ought to change how we dress to suit how other people might feel about us. Clothing can equip us to navigate the world, to level our footing, but when it comes down to it what I want to wear on a night out, or to the office, shouldn't be controlled by anything other than what I want it to reflect. How I choose to dress makes me feel confident and powerful. All that I have power over is how I feel.

The British style press is unique; we have a history of fashion magazines rooted in subculture. i-D has always been interested in people's style, not just their clothes, and I'm honoured to be a part of that legacy. We aren't particularly interested in consumable trends, on the shape of handbags or the shoe of the season. I do think that the energies of designers tend to align over a season's worth of collections – nobody creates in a bubble, and the best shows somehow reflect or challenge the world around us – but questions like 'are peplums trending?' Truly: who cares?

Life is full of what appear to be contradictions. I thought I was going to work in feminism and have ended up working in fashion. I'm a socialist who believes in high taxes, and I still love a Chanel handbag. Fashion has always been looked down upon as something ephemeral and shallow, but I think that a large part of that is because it's an industry centred around women and their bodies. The fashion that I'm most interested in is about self-expression, identity, community, desire, and embodying who you want to be in this world. **Sometimes I want to feel rich and powerful – two things which are inexorably interlinked in the world we live in – which is what carrying a Chanel handbag will do for me. As somebody who has worked to pay for it, that handbag feels good.**

I love to see women wearing clothes that amplify who they are: Lydia Lunch, Marlene Dietrich, Rihanna, Vivienne Westwood, in every incarnation of her identity – as a teacher, a designer, a punk. She really cared about women, about effecting change and doing what she felt was right in this world. She saw her clothes as a way of embodying her ideas and, in her words, 'confronting the rotten status quo through the way I dressed and dressed others'. In my opinion, nobody did it better.

The first piece I bought with my own money:

A Vivienne Westwood patent black handbag, quilted. I bought it with my student loan. I loved it because you could put it down in a club and wipe it down later, when it inevitably got sticky. It was big, super practical. I wish I still had it but it was made of vinyl and it got battered; it was never going to last for ever.

The one piece I'd save if my home was on fire:

There's so much I would try to save, but none of it is fashion. Although, that said, I'm very bad at saving and my collection of handbags is my pension. I can't afford to lose it!

ANITA PALLENBERG
on Inspiration

The embodiment of decadent, glamorous style, the Rolling Stones – and just about everybody else – have been influenced by Anita Pallenberg. Actress, artist, model and long-term partner of Keith Richards, German-Italian Anita came to epitomise the London look of the sixties. At fifty she went to study fashion at Central Saint Martins. This is an extract from an interview by Kira Jolliffe which appeared in *Cheap Date* magazine.

WHEN I WAS A LITTLE girl I was inspired by Cleopatra, and those drapey Greek goddess portraits that I saw in museums – I admired all of that. The film stars I liked were kind of mannish, but with great style, like Joan Crawford, say; the furs! The lipstick! I thought Barbara Stanwyck was really great. From the 60s I liked Anouk Aimée in *La Dolce Vita*; **she wore black shades, was kind of gender bender, and always dressed in black.** Jeanne Moreau, of course, and Delphine Seyrig too. There was a period then, with all these stylish women, not so obvious as Audrey Hepburn, who always wore Balenciaga and Givenchy, and it was not so much the name connected to the face, as the image that I admired. I didn't have much time for what was happening at Dior but Chanel always interested me – I always thought Coco Chanel very stylish. Of all the designers she was the only one who really understood comfort in a woman's body – for example, she did pockets. I can't live without pockets. She always did pockets.

RACHEL WEISZ
on Blue Denim

Oscar-winning actress, muse to Narciso Rodriguez and lifelong fan of vintage fashion, Rachel has worn some incredible clothes over the years, but denim remains her great love.

I HAVE WORN DENIM VIRTUALLY every day for many years. If I try to be unfaithful to (mostly blue) jeans, I no longer feel like myself. I think it's because jeans are the perfect combination of glamorous and practical. They carry so many associations: with rebellion and the spirit of youth culture, with respect for practical work versus a corporate office-based world. Jeans are right there at the heart of some of the most powerful moments in popular culture, from Elvis Presley singing 'Jailhouse Rock' to James Dean in *Rebel Without a Cause* or Marlon Brando in *The Wild One*.

Not that that I'm thinking about that when I pull on a pair of jeans or a denim jacket; I'm just getting dressed for the day. I live a privileged urban life, a long way from the rural workplaces where jeans were born. But they retain so much symbolic weight in our culture. They're special like that: simple and democratic but stylistically so rich. My favourite cut is probably a seventies-style slight flare. I love Levi's 501s but not so much on me.

One of the reasons I appreciate jeans is that they're signifiers of their historical moment. You can tell a pair of sixties bell-bottoms that someone might have worn at Woodstock from the disco denim of the seventies or the stonewashed ripped light-blue jeans of the eighties. That's partly because every subculture since the rebels of the fifties has adapted them for their own purpose.

167

Alongside that cultural storytelling, the fact that they're long-lasting and you can keep wearing them as they fade or fray means that they end up woven into your own personal story. When the knee rips, you can put a patch on it. When the hem frays you can cut it off . . . Jeans are endlessly customisable because they're tough and resilient. They become part of your journey.

I've always enjoyed the fact that blue jeans, which are almost the ultimate piece of Americana, were invented by Levi Strauss, a German immigrant, back in the nineteenth century. They're deeply associated with the United States' mythic sense of itself, with cowboys and outlaws as well as the hard-working men and women of the plains and the Midwest. Jeans were the ultimate symbol of Western freedom for kids in the Soviet Union before the fall of the Berlin Wall. And yet, like so many triumphs of American culture, they have their roots in immigration to the USA. I appreciate that about them, especially in these times of hostility to migrants both in the USA and in Europe. My parents were immigrants to London just before the Second World War, from Hungary and Austria respectively, so this element of the history is one that resonates with my personal story.

Jeans have been worn by male movie stars since the fifties, but I especially love women in jeans. Marilyn Monroe wore them in *The Misfits*, which was released in 1961 and is one of my favourite films. She took that extraordinary sexual swagger that Brando embodied in his Levi's and layered it on top of her own hyper-feminine sexuality. Our immediate associations with Marilyn and style might be the white halterneck dress over the air vent in *Seven Year Itch* or the body-skimming dresses and furs of *Some Like It Hot*, but for me her double denim paired with a crisp white shirt is her most seductive look of all. It was a genuinely subversive move for perhaps the most ultra-feminine movie star of them all, and she created a revolutionary piece of style inspiration for women.

I also love Lori Singer in *Footloose* from 1984, in blue jeans, belted and tucked into red cowboy boots, and a loose pink tie-front T-shirt with no bra . . . it just doesn't get more insouciant-sexy-cool than that. It's effortless, as if she just threw it all on. To look that fabulous in clothing that's available to everyone is so democratic, the very opposite of elitist or vain or try-hard.

Denim is now so mainstream that you can wear it to a fancy restaurant or in the boardroom but, even so, to choose jeans is to align yourself with a certain tribe. It still means something, especially as you age, especially as a woman. If you wear jeans into your seventies and eighties, you're identifying with a rebellious spirit, with the origins of the counter-culture.

Yves Saint Laurent said, 'I wish I had invented blue jeans: the most spectacular, the most practical, the most relaxed and nonchalant. They have modesty, sex appeal, simplicity . . . all I hope for in my clothes.' I can't possibly put it better. Jeans make me feel glamorous and cool. They will always have my heart.

The first pair of jeans I loved:

When I was about six I had a pair of blue denim dungarees with a 'Wow' patch sewn on the big front pocket. I wore them with a Wombles T-shirt.

The first piece I bought with my own money:

In the 1990s when I was starting to get acting jobs, I saved up for a skirt by Katharine Hamnett. It was black and long, almost to the ground, with a split up the back. You sort of hobbled when you walked, as the range of movement was quite restricted. I wore it with a big yellow sweatshirt.

169

The one piece I'd save if my home was on fire:

This is tricky. I have an Ossie Clark floral dress with a zip that snakes around your body. I don't think I could ever replace it, so perhaps I would save that. But then, I also have some dresses that Narciso Rodriguez made for me and they're definitely irreplaceable, so maybe those . . . Can I save them all?

HANIF KUREISHI
on Super-Painted Toenails

Following a serious fall in 2022 which immobilised him, Hanif Kureishi, Oscar-nominated playwright of *My Beautiful Laundrette* and prize-winning author of *The Buddha of Suburbia*, created a Substack entitled *The Kureishi Chronicles*, which was also published in installments on Twitter. An original version of the edited dispatch below was dictated from his hospital bed, shortly after his accident.

BEING A TETRAPLEGIC ISN'T ALL bad. As I write this, I am having a pedicure while eating caviar with a plastic spoon. My girlfriend is tickling me under the chin. I have just proposed to her. 'Barkis is willin''. While she pretends to contemplate the question - to my surprise, and that of most of my friends, who consider me to be less than a good catch, in fact a bad catch, and had advised me against proposing while I am in this condition — she eventually says yes, of course, and laughs.

As a kind of celebration, as I said, I'm having my first ever pedicure. The man doing the pedicure wears a sort of miner's harness on his forehead with a bright little torch attached. From where I am lying, with his whirring machine and his glasses covered in foot-dust, he resembles someone cleaning the inside of a nuclear dump.

I feel as if I am living in some sort of authoritarian regime in the hospital. Of course the people who work here are not tyrannical in any form. What I mean is that my body is constantly being invaded: someone comes in and shoves a tube into my ass; another nurse sticks a needle in my stomach; someone else inserts a needle in my arm. Then I am dragged in my bed to a

171

room at the far side of the hospital, where a complete stranger hits me over the head twenty times with a large magnetic ping-pong bat, for my own good. I feel like Jack Nicholson at the end of *One Flew Over the Cuckoo's Nest*, writhing in despair and helplessness.

I am feeling highly sartorial today. I am wearing my new white Snoopy socks, my black Uniqlo sports pants; on top, I have a long-sleeve Picasso T-shirt and, over that, an off-white Gap hoodie. On my head, I have an ochre woollen cap, of which I am proud. When I catch a glimpse of myself in any mirror, I am as enthusiastic and disappointed as any teenager.

I have been thinking a lot about my look, which is strange, since from the shoulders up I resemble a man who has just run out of a burning building – his own house. I am not crazy about the Uniqlo trousers, which are made of a strange, somewhat sticky, synthetic material. The sensation is a bit like wrapping bin liners around your legs and securing them at your stomach with a bit of old fraying rope. So this morning, as I lay on my back in the gym, and the physio was stretching me here and there, I was planning my next look, which Isabella can acquire for me on the streets of Rome.

During the physio, as I prepare for life as a married man, I am wondering what colour to paint my nails. The colours that I have suggested – which include the colours of my team Manchester United – have been considered by Isabella with some restrained hilarity.

Here in the hospital, I have seen a lot of Italian women – nurses, doctors, patients and visitors. Every day I see many nurses, but because they are wearing masks, I can only study their eyes, hair and eyebrows. I have to confess, I have acquired a knowledge of the Italian eyebrow which is extensive and detailed. Each eyebrow is, of course, a story and an artwork in itself. One of the nurses here, Roberta, who used to work in movies, in hair and make-up, told me that the eyebrow is the most important feature of the face. She added; the public might not notice it, but the eyebrow of the villain in any movie has to have special attention, as it must emphasise a 'wrong'un'.

I should stress here that the Italian male also attends to his eyebrows with calculated care. This is not something I have noticed in the British male. We are more primitive, except in British soap operas, where the male eyebrow seems to be given particular attention.

Italian women take good care of themselves. Everything about them is neat and planned, and the women who are not in work uniform — the visitors — dress brilliantly and vividly, both to express themselves, and to show others who they think they are. They wear a lot of clashing colours, which is very stylish, and confident.

When it comes to myself, who I am, and who I might become, I want to return to the late sixties and early seventies, when I was growing up. I guess most people of whatever age, wear the clothes of their youth. I will be doing this, with the volume turned up, and with super-painted toenails.

PART 5

DRESSING UP

'What I love are the possibilities . . . It's the same thing
in music and the same thing in acting and the same thing
in fashion. If I want to play this person,
I can become this person.'

ANDRÉ 3000, OUTKAST

JILLY COOPER
on Retail Therapy

With a career spanning several decades, 'Queen of the bonkbuster' Jilly Cooper continues to capture the hearts of readers through her unfiltered, unpretentious and absolutely unbeatable romcoms. In *Polo* she delves into the high society and even higher competition — both sporting *and* romantic — of a world replete with parties and polo matches.

HE PULLED WADS OF FRANCS out of his floppy shirt pocket. 'I've had a windfall at the casino. Let's go buy you some clothes.'

'The shops'll be shut,' protested Perdita.

'It's only half-past nine.' It seemed like midnight. 'We'll just catch them.'

They got to Yves St Laurent just as they were closing. Grace, Auriel and Chessie had all been excellent customers over the years so the manageress was quite prepared to stay open and even produced a bottle of champagne. Red lounged like some sultan on a white sofa smoking a long cigar, drinking very slowly and totally dominating Perdita's choice.

With that waterfall of hair and strange unicorn looks and body undulating like an ox-bow river, he wanted her starkly plain, mostly in blacks, navy blues and bottle greens, with the occasional brilliant cyclamen, purple of kingfisher-blue. Everything had to fit perfectly and if it didn't it was kept back to be taken in or up. Perdita, who always wanted everything at once, grumbled like hell. But she was in a state of frantic excitement and arousal.

Red, used to accompanying Grace and Auriel to fashion shows, was an expert on line and cut. He enjoyed watching Perdita's voluptuous pleasure as she swayed and preened in front of him. He liked the way she quivered as he slowly ran his hand over her breasts or her belly, testing the smoothness of the fit.

After an hour and a half, when they'd bought almost the entire shop, he told her to put on a pair of black high heels and an ivy-green taffeta dress, clinging and high-necked at the front, plunging to the base of her spine at the back.

As she came out, having piled up her hair with a dark green sequinned comb given her by the manageress, she found Red examining the contents of some little boxes a jeweller had rushed in from next door. From one he drew out a necklace and drop-earrings in huge, very dark sapphires. 'These'll do. Come here,' he ordered Perdita.

Very slowly he put them round her neck and hooked them on to her ears. All trace of her tears had gone now. The sapphires and the ivy-green taffeta heightened her white skin and made her strange eyes so dark that they seemed all pupil.

'You'll do,' he said.

'You can't give me all this,' said Perdita. 'I hate you.'

Red laughed. 'With enemies like me, who needs friends? **One must sapphire to be beautiful.**' Then, when she tried to protest, murmured: 'Don't spoil it.'

He paid for the lot out of his casino winnings. He'd call tomorrow and tell the manageress where the rest had to be sent.

AJ TRACEY
on Diamonds

AJ is a rapper, singer, songwriter and record producer whose self-titled debut album was a massive critical and commercial success in 2019. He was brought up in Ladbroke Grove and says his style is very West London, via the Bronx. AJ's significant collection of chains now lives mostly in a safe but, as a self-confessed addict, he's not giving up on jewellery any time soon.

I STARTED GETTING INTERESTED IN fashion when I was about ten. It began with trainers. Like most kids my age, I was obsessed with football. I really wanted some Total 90s, which were football boots with little studs. I asked my mum for them. We didn't have a lot of money when I was growing up so she didn't exactly go out and buy me everything off the long list of things I required, but I did get those football boots. I wore them all the time, so that I was always ready for any impromptu game of football.

I tend to dress for my mood so, for example, if I'm wearing a black Nike tracksuit and black Air Forces, I'm probably in a bad mood; whereas when I'm in a good mood I'll be in something a bit more fly, a bit groovy. I like to wear traditional streetwear, a baseball jacket and some Nike Airs, but I want those Airs to be loud, maybe animal print, so they're funky. You need to go a little bit wild. That fly look is very West London.

I'm heavily influenced by classic old-school hip-hop, by early Bronx style, so original Jordan 1s, for example. Also British punk bands like the Sex Pistols. I love Japanese denim. Kapital and Engineered Garments are some of my favourite brands at the moment. Japanese designers are really good at taking a concept and making it their own. Kapital does classic American cowboy-style denim but in these amazing fabrics. The level of detail is incredible. Or a pair of fatigued cargo pants from Engineered Garments; you can't just throw them on, there's too much care that's gone into them.

I started getting into rapping when I was about six years old, and I begged my mum for a chain. I kept begging for years, and then on my eighteenth birthday she gave me a little silver chain that she'd saved up for. I loved it. I wore it every day, didn't take it off. Then when I started making my own money, aged about twenty-three, I bought myself a white gold chain with a pendant in the shape of a Cupid heart, with pink sapphires. I couldn't afford to put diamonds in it yet, but I don't regret it because I really loved that chain.

Over the next few years, every time I made some money from a new mixtape or a tour, I bought myself another chain. They were like trophies. My next one was yellow gold. The pendant was in the shape of a backpack because in hip hop, the phrase 'getting to bag' means 'getting to the money'. The bag had rubies on the front and diamonds around the bag on the back plate. I also took my old heart pendant back to the jeweller and got the arrow covered in diamonds. I don't really see people upgrading their chains but it made sense to me because why am I getting a new chain if I can upgrade this one that I still love?

My AJ Tracey chain came next. It weighs about 380 grams. The pendant is embossed with my logo in diamonds. When my older brother opened the box he said, 'I'm not going to lie, that's beautiful. But it's ridiculous. Where are you going to wear it?' He was right. I did wear it for a while, out on the street, to prove to myself that I wasn't scared. But London's a devious place and, really and truly, wearing it didn't prove I was tough; it just proved I'm a little bit stupid. Though I've still got it, by god's grace!

After that I went out and got a bust down watch. A 'bust down' in the culture means it's completely busted down with diamonds. The watch had been taken apart, broken down, drilled into and had diamonds put into it. I recently sold it. The thing is, it's worth less than you'd think because only another rapper is going to want it. Watch collectors don't want a piece that's had holes drilled into it like that.

Then came my 'Ladbroke Grove' chain, to commemorate my song. **It's made of white and rose gold infinity links, and again, loads of diamonds. It's ridiculously heavy. After an hour, my neck's going to be hurting.**

I've recently put them all away in a safe, along with the Rolex I bought myself for my birthday. I made a decision not to wear my jewellery any more because I don't want any negative energy or symbols of the politics of the street coming into contact with the people I love. For me, my jewellery has always represented my achievements but that's not how other people see it. For them it says that I think I'm better than them. I didn't realise until I grew up a bit, but there are people like me, coming from the same background, who are looking at me in all my chains and thinking, why aren't you helping us instead of shitting on us?

I haven't given up my jewellery and I'm sure I'll buy another chain at some point because it's like an addiction, but I feel I've come full circle. Almost like, I've got it out of my system.

These days I wear the chains if I'm making a video, but day to day, the only thing I wear is an Apple watch.

A stylish person is someone whose style you can appreciate, even if it's not to your taste. I liken it to music. I might not be a fan of a certain track or genre but I can say, 'That's not for me but I appreciate it'. Same thing with clothes.

Skepta is super stylish, so is ASAP Rocky. Andre 3000 is the GOAT. He's an icon. **And an honourable mention to Princess Diana. She always looked amazing.**

The first piece I bought with my own money:

A New Era cap. It was an army camouflage one and it had eyes on it. I bought it from a little shop in the Queensway mall that sold American clothes, and I took it home feeling very proud of myself. My mum knew I'd gone to buy it but my dad didn't and when he saw the cap he was like, 'Nah. You're not wearing that.' Because where I come from, that was a gang-affiliated hat. He made me take it back!

The one piece I'd save if my home was on fire:

I have a pair of Air Max 90s by Off-White, one of the first to drop. Virgil sent them to me, and he wrote 'pasta' on the side, for my song 'Pasta', which was how he came to know about me. We got talking and he sent me a few things over the years. He was such a lovely person and now of course he's gone, so those shoes are very sentimental for me.

CHARLOTTE TILBURY
on Glamour

Charlotte Tilbury, MBE is a beauty entrepreneur and has been spreading the magic of confidence-boosting make-up for more than thirty years. She's created trend-setting looks at Prada, Alexander McQueen, Chloé, Lanvin and many others. She has 100 *Vogue* covers to her name and is the go-to creator of wearable, luxury-finish glamour for countless celebrities. She developed products for luxury brands before launching her own make-up and skincare ranges in 2013, which have earned her the undying loyalty of millions of fans. Her award-winning Magic Cream is the moisturiser to the stars and one is sold every minute around the world, while one of her Pillow Talk products is sold every six seconds globally.

I LEARNED ABOUT THE POWER of clothes and make-up early in my life thanks to my parents. I was born in London but brought up in Ibiza during the 1970s and 1980s. My mother worked in fashion and my father was an artist. Clothes and style, interiors and art mattered to them very much. They had a huge appreciation of beautiful things, as do I. They were also very sociable and there were always a lot of people around, many of whom were musicians, artists, writers, designers and actors. Ibiza was very multicultural back then and very rebellious. It was wild. People dressed as if they were straight off a film set, with crazy hats and diamante wigs and punked-up ball gowns. It was all hugely inspiring for me and has stayed in my head as a library of images.

My father taught me about colour theory. Being a painter, he was acutely aware of how to deploy colour, and that showed up in his clothes as well as his pictures. He wore bright-pink espadrilles and would clash colours beautifully. I used that knowledge when I began to work as a make-up artist. I was barely out of my teens but I had a clear sense of which colour would make green eyes pop, which was going to work with blue eyes or brown . . .

My father also said that everything in life is made up of light and shade and I really learned the truth of that when I was working with photographers and cinematographers on shoots. The way they use pink light to create a glow around a model, for example, and silver reflectors under their face to throw light around. I channelled all that knowledge into the development of products like my Hollywood Flawless Filter.

Observing the creative process behind a shoot, I noticed the way designers, stylists, photographers and fashion directors drew on a wide range of visual references - from vintage movie posters to crafts and paintings or pieces from a fashion archive. And yet I saw the same archetypes and icons cropping up over and over again: the bombshell, say, or the sophisticate; David Bowie or Marilyn Monroe. What made a look interesting was the contemporary twist.

It was thinking about a way I could harness what I'd learned from luxury fashion and beauty into the creation of a range of accessible products, that led me to come up with my ten iconic make-up looks, from the rock chick to the starlet. I realised that creating personal style was all about identifying your tribes and vibes, drawing on the power of all those icons who have dared to express themselves and become a resource for us to refer to. You don't have to stick to one look, of course. We're all multi-faceted people and we switch between roles all the time. I might decide that I'll be the sophisticate at a big meeting, and then the bombshell at a party later that night.

As you get more experienced and confident, you learn about a range of visual references but you also learn what works for you and what doesn't. Sometimes that's a question of body shape or colouring. I'm very curvy, for example, so I don't wear boxy jackets because I just end up looking like a box! I have very pale skin and bright auburn hair. I look a bit painterly, a bit pre-Raphaelite. I can wear a lot of bright colours.

There are certain style elements I come back to over and over again because of how they make me feel. I love the Stevie Nicks look, chiffon capes and diamante – old-school film star but rock and roll. I still find it really helpful to ask myself, how can I take something from the past and make it modern? Perhaps a piece of vintage clothing, but clashed with something from a different period. Perhaps a classic dress but I rock it up, put a men's jacket with it. I will see how a piece can be brought into my style, by adapting it to work with what I have already.

Some of what you learn is quite intangible. You just feel more powerful in tailoring or high heels, more comfortable in black and white or in clashing print. High heels, for example. I love them, wear them all the time. I've got heels for the office and for parties but also heels for the beach and for going up mountains! I stand differently if I'm wearing heels. They just make me feel great. Longer, leaner, more fabulous.

It's different for everyone, but once you've found it, follow that sense of euphoria. I think most of us have felt that sense of delight that a perfect new dress can give you: like Christmas Eve on the inside. The elements of style are a language of self-expression. **Fashion, clothes, make-up, hair and fragrance should never be trivialised because style, at its best, is about creating and harnessing a glimmer of light, of magic. It's about energy.** If you feel confident, you can be confident. You can use personal style to create a virtuous circle of positivity that empowers you as an individual and radiates out to create change in the world. It's a magical chain reaction.

To be stylish you have to be prepared to stand out, to look a little different. But I've learned that a stylish look doesn't have to be outrageous. It just needs an unexpected element, a twist that makes something really personal for you. It's different from fashion. You risk being a fashion victim if you follow trends too closely at the expense of what feels right for you. Style is about wearing what you love so that you feel like the best version of yourself.

For me, it comes back to glamour. One of the definitions of the word is 'enchantment', that idea of 'casting a spell over the world'. This is the glamour I love. It doesn't necessarily mean wearing a ball gown or a plunging swimsuit. **You can be glamorous in whatever way you want – in jeans, a man's jacket, a red lip and a diamond necklace. Glamour glistens like a little bit of magic.** To be glamorous is to sparkle, in whatever way works for you.

I've noticed that the people who work with me have ended up dressing more and more glamorously. I never make any demands on my staff as to what they should wear; it's more a contagious thing. It's like the hostess at the party – if she dances, the guests will dance, too. But for glamour (or any style) to be powerful, it has to be completely democratic and authentic. I believe that everybody should be who they want to be.

At every stage of my career I've wanted to harness the most cutting-edge developments in the cosmetics industry. The technology now is incredible, and as Arthur C. Clarke, science fiction writer, inventor and undersea explorer, said, 'Any sufficiently advanced technology is indistinguishable from magic.' Glamour is magical and energetic. It radiates from people. We are all energetic beings, transmitting good vibes or bad. When we are as positive as we can be, wonderful things happen for us and around us, to us and to others. Anything that can help us switch our mindset, so we see opportunities rather than problems, so that we co-create rather than tear down, is a wonderful resource. **That's what style is for me. It's a little bit of magic. A little bit of love.**

DAVINA MCCALL
on Lingerie

Davina is a television broadcaster, bestselling author, online fitness instructor and menopause campaigner. She spends at least half her waking hours in work-out gear, but whether she's wearing leggings or a party dress, style always starts with her underwear.

WOMEN'S EXPECTATIONS ABOUT THEIR LINGERIE are very different in France from in Britain. French women expect to see women of all ages in lingerie adverts. And they expect to remain visible and to be admired throughout their lives, whether they're pregnant, ageing or elderly. This is not about male attention. It's about wanting to be seen, on their own terms. Women give other women attention in France. And it means that French women glow. I think we all deserve to feel like that. My mother was French, very attractive and always wore beautiful lingerie, as did my older sister, who spent all her money on gifts for her friends and exquisite underwear for herself. So I grew up with those role models.

My good mood begins in the morning with the first thing I put against my skin. I choose underwear that will cheer me up, make me feel confident, powerful. I have a wardrobe of lingerie in different colours, fabrics and styles to suit my moods. The only thing they have in common is that they're all matching sets. This is a rule as far as I'm concerned: my underwear must match!

When I have an important meeting, I will wear my 'I mean business' underwear. The best of the best, which I know is going to make me feel like a million dollars and totally kick-ass. The bra is a soft golden colour and the straps have three delicate gold chains hanging in loops over my shoulders. I wear a matching thong with its three little chains dangling above a cut-out at the base of my spine. This is highly impractical underwear – you can feel the chains – but that's precisely why I like it. It feels like self-love and self-respect.

When I have to wear a basic, flesh-coloured, seamless and invisible pair of knickers for work, I can practically feel them sapping my confidence and positivity. A flesh-coloured seamless thong is designed to leave no trace on the clothed body but it definitely leaves a trace on my sense of who I am. I end up feeling highly self-conscious.

I used to save the good stuff for special occasions and saucy time. **It was only when I was in my early forties, going through the perimenopause and feeling invisible in a society that barely sees older women, that I realised the everyday power of great underwear.** Like many women in midlife, I worried that I had become irrelevant. I felt invisible, and so I dressed in the blandest, most neutral way possible: jeans, jumper, boots, on repeat. A baggy T-shirt for summer.

Then I realised that I didn't want to live like that any more. I started looking for inspiration and found a group on Facebook called 'Fifty AF'. They were the most badass fifty-plus women with a zero-fucks mentality, all posting the most hilarious memes and photos of themselves looking hot while wearing whatever the hell they wanted. It was so refreshing. I knew I wanted to be in that club, embodying the spirit of 'let's not go quietly'.

So I made a decision to change how I thought about ageing, and myself. Now I wear amazing underwear every day. I've got a collection of ridiculous sunglasses . . . I've got hats, neckerchiefs, scarves. You name it, if it's an accessory, I'm into it. I dress to be seen, primarily by myself but also by others – especially women going through a similar phase of life.

Lingerie can be as personal as any other aspect of style. It

Style and Substance

doesn't have to be outrageous but there is an association with sex and sexiness, of course, which I enjoy. I love a sheer bra, for example. But the thing about sexy underwear is that it's not the underwear that's sexy, it's the woman who's wearing it. For many of us who only wear our good underwear when we know it will be taken off, wearing that lingerie is an act of foreplay. It signals intent, to yourself and your partner. It makes you feel great.

Why would you save that feeling for best, or for others? It's great to look sexy for your partner (men, please take note, this applies to you too — no grey baggy cotton pants full of holes, please!) but it's even better to look and feel fabulous for yourself. Yesterday was a quiet day. I was working; I wasn't going to see my boyfriend. I needed to be comfortable in underwear that didn't show through my clothes, but I also wanted the spark and the glow that comes from knowing I'd chosen something beautiful, just for me.

Wearing great lingerie is an act of personal affirmation and it's available for everyone. I know many older or larger women who embody this; I know disabled women who are glowing with self-acceptance and dress accordingly. I see those women in their beautiful underwear and they are so attractive. Because they FEEL it.

I know it's not easy. When I was thinner and my skin was smooth, my boobs were pert and my knees weren't baggy, even when I was wearing pretty undies I felt embarrassed and negative about my body and my being. Now, most of the time, I love my body and myself. Lingerie has been part of that work, of building myself up.

These days, lingerie brands show their products on women of all shapes and sizes, which is a positive but too recent change. It really helps to show women that everybody can look beautiful in beautiful underwear. Lingerie is a tool in your mission to learn to be comfortable in your skin. Wear whatever it is that appeals to you. It doesn't have to be expensive; there are great-value brands around. **Start with an elevated basic: a black bra with a little lace. Go matching. See how that makes you feel** . . . Then just keep exploring. After all, with underwear as with any clothes, you are sexy if you feel sexy and stylish if you feel stylish.

Before I got clean at the age of twenty-four, I was a drug addict and so full of shame and self-loathing that style was the last thing on my mind. I didn't have enough money to put petrol in my car or buy food, my boyfriend had left and I was sleeping on a camp bed back at my dad's. I was a mess, and I hated myself for what I'd become. But when I got clean, simply waking up in dry sheets was a miracle. Those mornings reminded me what it felt like to be at peace with myself. **I have never lost that sense of wonder at waking to a bright new day of life rather than a fog of shame and self-hatred. I still feel grateful, and I celebrate every single morning with the loveliest lingerie I can find.**

PENELOPE TREE
on Going to the Ball

With her wide eyes and long hair Penelope Tree became one of the most iconic models of the sixties. This is the story of the night she was discovered. In 2024 she will publish her first novel, *Piece of My Heart*.

NEW YORK CITY, 1962

BEFORE I EVEN CAUGHT SIGHT of him, the sound of his voice – petulant, campy and brimming with self-confidence – shocked and thrilled me. Across the drawing room, surrounded by a cluster of couture-clad goddesses, this strange flamboyant creature was recounting a salacious anecdote about a Greek shipping magnate whose wife had died in mysterious circumstances.

Knowing I was a fan, my mother had informed me earlier that Truman Capote was coming to the lunch party she was giving for her friends, Bill and Babe Paley.

Though I was a bolshy, ungainly twelve-year-old and an indifferent student, I'd been an avid reader from an early age. Not to imply I understood everything I read – I didn't – but since Mr Capote's books were written in a deceptively simple style, I had recently devoured *Other Voices, Other Rooms*, *The Grass Harp*, *Breakfast at Tiffany's*, and *A Christmas Story*, about his childhood in Monroeville, Alabama.

I'd also learned he was the inspiration behind Dill, Scout's neighbour and best friend in Harper Lee's *To Kill a Mockingbird* which I'd studied at school and loved. In fact, Mr Capote's inner world was so present and alive in my imagination, that presumptuously or not, I felt that he and I were already friends.

191

When lunch was announced, I hung back as the ladies sailed into the dining room. He spied me lurking and said hello. Soon I was red-faced, clumsily declaring my love for his work. More than anything in the world, I confided, I wanted to be a writer too. What was his advice?

Thankfully, Mr Capote didn't give me the brush-off, and insisted I sat next to him at lunch, disrupting the placement to my mother's annoyance. I can't claim he and I became intimates, but he was encouraging, funny, and treated me like an adult. I sent him some stories I had written, and he replied kindly, telling me to keep writing every day no matter what. 'Talent means nothing if you don't put in the work.' Since the age of eleven, he told me, he had written for at least three hours every day.

Four years passed. While I was weathering a stormy adolescence, Mr Capote had become the most acclaimed writer in America following the publication of his true crime novel *In Cold Blood*.

To celebrate his success, he invited, as he sardonically put it, 'five hundred of my closest friends' to attend a Black and White Dance at the Plaza Hotel. For months beforehand, Mr Capote taunted those around him; 'Maybe you'll be invited, maybe you won't.' To my amazement, I *was* invited, along with my parents and sister Frankie.

Immediately I started dreaming about my dress. As a huge fan of the Alvin Ailey Dance Theatre, and modern dance in general, I was inspired by what dancers wore, both on and off stage. Even though I'd never even taken a dance class, I practically lived in the Capezio shop. But it turned out they didn't make one-off designs for civilians so I had to think again. At the time, Paraphernalia was the only boutique in New York that came close to rivalling Biba in London. The in-house designer, super talented Betsey Johnson, had only recently graduated from Pratt. She too was obsessed with dance clothes and enthused about creating a completely unique look for the Ball. We discussed various ideas and agreed immediately on the material for the dress: black silk jersey, because of the fluid way it moves, and because it fits the body like a second skin.

Just a few days later I was summoned to her studio for a fitting. When I changed from my school clothes and looked in the mirror, **I absolutely knew in my bones that this dress was going to change my life.** Betsey had radically rejigged the leotard look we'd originally envisaged, transforming it into a simple master-piece that far, far exceeded my expectations.

The dress was backless to the waist and held in place by the skinniest of spaghetti straps criss-crossed once between my shoulder blades and fastened invisibly on both sides of the skirt under my arms. The front of the dress had two side slits origin-ating from just under the bust (I went braless) reaching all the way to the ground, so my bare midriff was visible on either side of a long panel down the front, and completely exposed when I walked. I wore my hip-hugging Capezio tights underneath, and black ballet slippers as always. The black jersey mask was designed to echo the V-shaped neckline. Like a mermaid's tail to a mermaid, both mask and dress felt entirely natural, as if they were part of me.

Getting my parents' approval to wear such a revealing outfit might have been a problem — it was nearly sixty years ago after all — but they were both preoccupied and didn't see the dress on me until the night of the Ball, as they were heading out to a dinner. As I remember, my father was busy trying to prevent an enormous headdress of coq feathers and diamonds from sliding off my mother's head, and they were already late. After a shocked double take in my direction, they departed, having instructed me to meet them by the cloakroom near the Plaza ballroom at 10.15 p.m.

When the car pulled up outside the Central Park South entrance, my heart started hammering with alarm at the sight of the klieg lights illuminating a red carpet walkway. Though it was a cold and rainy night, scores of onlookers were gathered behind police barriers, while journalists and TV crews were jostling about, filming the arriving guests. I hid behind a beautiful girl in tall fluffy bunny ears, who turned out to be Candice Bergen. Someone in the crowd yelled out, 'This schtick is inappropriate when there's a war going on.' Candice Bergen's date shot back 'The WAR is inappropriate!' 'Bring on the tumbrils' someone else shouted. Finally I made it inside and flowed up the stairs with a slow-moving stream of extravagantly attired masked guests.

After reuniting with my parents and sister, we joined the queue to greet our host and his guest of honour, Kay Graham, who received us all just inside the entrance of the candlelit ballroom. Mr Capote was cordial though he appeared somewhat detached. 'I'm so glad you could come,' he repeated five hundred and forty times. Apparently there had been some last-minute additions to the guest list, including a woman who had threatened suicide if she and her husband didn't receive an invitation.

On the far side of the dance floor, Peter Duchin's orchestra was already in full swing. To my ears, the music was oldies fare — show tunes and Cole Porter — but delivered in the most swellegant way imaginable. **The entire ballroom was already heaving with feathered species of all kinds; birds of paradise kissing birds of prey, their jewelled eyes glinting in the dim light, everyone chirping, 'You look marvellous, darling.'**

My parents disappeared into the thicket, so I peeled off, enveloped inside a cloak of invisibility; one of the perks of wearing a mask. Now, decades on, the exact sequence of events eludes me, but at various moments I watched Jerome Robbins waltzing with Lauren Bacall and witnessed Norman Mailer loudly insulting an older man (who turned out to be McGeorge Bundy, National Security Advisor to President Johnson, and one of the architects of the Vietnam War). I also spied Mia Farrow dancing with a bodyguard as Frank Sinatra looked on; a distinctly uneasy expression on his face. Then I came across a party of plainly dressed

Style and Substance

folk sitting at a large round table, staring in amazement at their ornately opulent surroundings. From numerous articles in the press at the time, I gathered they were the Texans Mr Capote had befriended while writing *In Cold Blood*. The group included Alvin Dewey, the detective who had tracked down the Clutter family's killers. Consequently, I felt the Stetson-hatted Mr Dewey was by far the most glamorous figure in the room.

Having flitted about on my own for hours, an unlikely white knight appeared in the form of Cecil Beaton, who, without a word, grasped my hand and led me to the dance floor. He was a wonderful dancer, and I was grateful he had noticed me, but after a couple of numbers he bowed and disappeared into the crowd. Shortly afterwards my father appeared, beckoning frantically. Even the party of the century was not going to interfere with his usual bedtime.

We were back home in pumpkinville by midnight. I took off clothes and make-up thinking, 'well that's that', and went to sleep, somewhat disappointed my hunch about the life-changing dress had been so patently misjudged.

Then, at nine o'clock the next morning the phone rang, and an unfamiliar voice roared down the line; 'Penelope darling, this is Diana Vreeland from *Vogue*. Dick Avedon and I saw you last night looking absolutely *ravishing*, and wondered if you would consider doing some test shots for us?' And with those words, for better and for worse, the future opened up before me.

As for Mr Capote, I saw him only two more times in the years leading up to his death, when he was clearly unwell. I regret not having the life skills to understand how much he was suffering and beat a hasty retreat on both occasions. He remains my childhood hero, for his extraordinary body of work, and for the person he was when I first met him, the man behind the mask.

ZAINAB JIWA
on Hijabs and High Fashion

Zainab is a digital artist, online presenter and style obsessive. At university she was the only fashion student wearing a hijab and she's been described online as the 'hijabi cosplay creator'. In 2023 she hosted TikTok's coverage of the BAFTA award ceremony, wearing an epic monochrome gown with a train, elbow-length gloves and a matching hijab.

MY HEADSCARF HAS BECOME A key element of how I present myself, almost like a style signature, but it's been an interesting journey getting to this place. I loved fancy dress as a child, though I dressed my dolls more than myself because when my family arrived in the UK we didn't have a lot of money. I was born in Kenya and I was four when we came to London. My heritage is both African and sixth-generation Indian. My mum wears a hijab, as do my sisters, so it was a very normal thing for me; I knew I wanted to wear it. I was also really into clothes, and that did create a bit of tension for me when I started wearing the hijab. I've learned how to express myself alongside the hijab now but when I was younger I used to see it as a hindrance. I would put together an outfit and then be annoyed that I had to wear the hijab on top, which kind of ruined the look. Now I see it as a challenge to express my individuality alongside my identity. The headscarf becomes an extra element to add to the mix, adding to the playfulness. I really enjoy it. **I'm dressing to elevate my individuality *within* my identity.**

I'm quite a theatrical and flamboyant dresser, which I think comes directly from both my Indian and African cultural heritage. The women in my community and back in Kenya wear bold prints and heavy colour and bright jewellery. I fell in love with that maximalist vibe.

My mum has been my number one inspiration. She loves to dress up. She hosts parties at our place for friends and family and I love to see her in a ton of jewellery and a beautiful sari, in her element, full of confidence. At our mosque, which we dress up to visit, she's known as the Sari Lady because she never wears anything else. I see how dressing up to go out or have people over transforms her energy and builds her confidence. It's a way of stepping into her power, and that has been a wonderful thing for me to witness.

I feel extremely powerful when I wear what I want. If I look good, I feel good, and if I feel good, I do good. When my sisters say to me, 'Isn't it uncomfortable, wearing heels all day?' I explain that it isn't a problem. I love heels, they make me feel great, and that means I can get out there and do my job as well as I possibly can. They're worth it.

Rawdah Mohamed, who's a Somali-Norwegian hijab-wearing model and fashion editor at *Vogue* Scandinavia, is a huge inspiration to me. She uses amazing sculptural pieces to frame her body, lots of colour and pattern, and whatever she's wearing she carries herself amazingly. I've been experimenting with different ways to tie my hijab thanks to her. I also watch Bollywood films and take inspiration from the costumes, especially the accessories. I'm really into earrings and tend to wear big beaded Indian earrings at parties and to red carpet events. I might wear a gown or Western suit and add Indian earrings or a headpiece. Indian women are the queens of accessorising.

Mainstream pop culture is where I find my ideas for cosplay creations, especially superhero films. I don't see any Muslims in those films, and I didn't see myself in them either until I started putting myself into those clothes. Wearing a Spiderman bodysuit with my hijab, for example, allowed me to see myself as a character, a hero.

I love to stage recreations of my favourite characters. It's my way of paying tribute to the costume designers, because for me their work is an artform. When the Barbie film was being promoted and images were coming out of what Margot Robbie was wearing, I staged some pictures. I couldn't not. Dressing my Barbie dolls was what first got me into fashion, and I've loved pink ever since I was a child. As far as I'm concerned if you don't like pink as an adult, you need to grow up! It's such a flattering and versatile colour, for men and women, and that bubble-gum aesthetic really appeals. Cosplay is pure creativity and escapism but all fashion is about escaping the everyday.

As a movie and TV geek, I feel so fortunate to have a job that means I'm invited to attend premieres and red carpet events, and as a fashion girl I can't believe I get to work with stylists and designers to put together incredible outfits. For any big event, I aspire to look elegant but with a bit of bite. I'm quite conceptual rather than instinctive in the way I think about outfits, partly because of my love of costume and partly because I studied fashion and visual culture at university. I do put a lot of thought into what I'm wearing. When I hosted the BAFTA ceremony for TikTok, I curated that outfit really carefully. I worked with stylist Hanaa Heetun and upcoming designer Sara Hegyi. She made me a slim high-necked jumpsuit, very fitted and cinched at the waist, in this incredible white and dark grey fabric that was inspired by the inkblot tests used by psychologists. I wanted to draw on an image from science and take it into a creative and artistic space. Over the jumpsuit, I wore a huge skirt with a long train, all in the same fabric. We figured out a way I could gather the train up and tuck it away so I could run around on the red carpet, and then unfurl it again. I had a matching deep-grey hijab, and I wore elbow-length white gloves with lots of rings over the top. And big round mirror earrings, which I found in Italy the week before. I'm very drawn to mirrored elements, because they're a playful reference to vanity but they also speak to self-reflection. There was quite a lot going on, and Hanaa and I thought about each element carefully, trying to bring a touch of playfulness and surrealism into the outfit. The vibe we were going for was 'superhero goes to the ball'. It was great fun.

There definitely is a tension between modesty and fashion, or being less visible and very visible. There are always conversations about that in my community and I speak a lot about it, because it's such an important topic. My flamboyant colours and accessories do go against the grain of modest dressing. I acknowledge and own that, but both modesty and style depend on how you perceive them; there is no set way to do either. Religion is deeply personal and when it comes to the religious idea of modesty, I show modesty by covering my body and my hair. That is how I like to cover up, to express my identity, my religion and myself. For me, modesty does not mean wearing all black. My family is really supportive of me and my exploration of style. They're also really grounding. I speak to my sisters every day and they give me feedback. They'll say, 'You might need to cover up a little more next time', if I've got carried away with a costume design, for example. **In the wider community there will always be some people who disapprove but it's a conversation, one I'm glad to be taking part in.**

Style is having a creative eye. You can have all the money in the world and still have no style. It's super subjective, of course, but as long as your style is a form of self-expression and expresses your attitude to life and the world, the content is not important. John Berger said that we never look at one thing in isolation, we always see it in its context. For me, fashion is that one thing in isolation, whereas style is what you choose, what you take from fashion and how you combine it with other elements. I find the subjectivity very liberating. If everyone is going to see you in the context they've made for themselves, according to their ways of seeing, there's no point in thinking too much about their reactions.

You just choose what makes you feel great. Then you'll be stylish.

The first piece I bought with my own money:

I sold one of my digital artworks when I was barely into secondary school, so I had some money of my own for the first time. I went to Topshop and bought myself a skater dress. Crazy, because I couldn't wear it: it was short and I don't show my legs. But I loved it, I wanted to own it, so I bought it and then I figured out how to wear it — with wide-leg trousers. That was my first step into fashion.

The one piece I'd save if my home was on fire:

My hijab. I could be wearing a rubbish sack but so long as I also had the headscarf, I could style an outfit. I'd still be me.

PATTI SMITH
on Fancy Dress

Legendary singer-songwriter, punk-rock performer, visual artist and writer, Patti Smith won a National Book Award for her memoir *Just Kids*, an evocative, honest and moving coming-of-age story of her extraordinary relationship with the artist Robert Mapplethorpe.

WE WERE INVITED TO A fancy dress ball hosted by Fernando Sánchez, the great Spanish designer known for his provocative lingerie. Loulou and Maxime sent me a vintage gown of heavy crepe designed by Schiaparelli. The top was black, with poufed sleeves and a V-neck bodice, sweeping down into a red floor-length skirt. It looked suspiciously like the dress Snow White was wearing when she met the Seven Dwarfs. Robert was beside himself. 'Are you going to wear it?' he said excitedly.

Lucky for me, it was too small. Instead, I dressed completely in black, finishing it off with pristine white Keds. David and Robert were in black tie. This was one of the most glamorous parties of the season, attended by the upper echelon of art and fashion. I felt like a Buster Keaton character, leaning alone against a wall when Fernando came up. He took me in skeptically.

'Darling, the ensemble is fabulous,' he said, patting my hand, eyeing my black jacket, black tie, black silk shirt, and heavily pegged black satin pants, **'but I'm not so sure about the white sneakers.'**

'But they're essential to my costume.'

'Your costume? What are you dressed as?'

'A tennis player in mourning.'

Fernando looked me up and down and began to laugh.   *201*

'Perfect,' he said, showing me off to the room. He took my hand and immediately led me to the dance floor. Being from South Jersey, I was now in my element. The dance floor was mine.

Fernando was so intrigued by our exchange that he gave me a slot in his upcoming fashion show. I was invited to join the lingerie models. I wore the same black satin pants, a tattered T-shirt, the white sneakers, modeling his eight-foot-long black feather boa and singing 'Annie Had a Baby'. It was my catwalk debut, the beginning and end of my modeling career.

ANAÏS NIN
on Adopting a Mask

Though her writing was largely ignored for years, in 1966, when Anaïs Nin was sixty-three, she published *The Diary of Anaïs Nin*. The epic seven-volume work spanned fifty years and made her a feminist icon.

I STOOD IN DARK SPACE, dressed luxuriously in brocades and jewels, like a Byzantine idol. I wore a tiara of precious stones. I stood like an idol. People said: 'She is a resplendent idol but not a human being.'

. . . Allendy said the dream did not represent a fear but a wish. I wished to be an idol. What was the characteristic of an idol? Invulnerability. As an idol I intimidated or ruled over people. I preserved myself from pain. It was to conceal my softness, and my purity and my simplicity. It was a mask. Aggressively dazzling in self-protection. The first day I came to see Allendy I wore a draped costume and a byzantine [sic] hat, and I succeeded in intimidating him by my strangeness. The Antinea [sic] of the Atlantis. A desire to be more interesting, more accentuated. A role. I played the role of a sophistication which was not truly my own. In all this he seemed so right. **I began to see how much of an armor my costumes had been.**

SANDY POWELL
on Making a Character

Sandy Powell is a multi-award-winning costume designer who has worked in theatre and film since the 1980s. Some of her notable work includes the glam-rock camp of *Velvet Goldmine* with Ewan McGregor, the lush historical fantasy of Sally Potter's *Orlando*, 1950s American elegance in *Carol* starring Cate Blanchett, a vision of Manhattan in the late nineteenth century for *Gangsters of New York* directed by Martin Scorsese and the uncanny period detail of *The Favourite*, starring Olivia Colman and Rachel Weisz. In 2022 she was awarded a BAFTA fellowship, the only costume designer ever to have been honoured in this way. She has worn many gowns on the red carpet but these days she mostly wears men's suits and boots. She has bright-orange hair.

COSTUME IS ABOUT TELLING STORIES and creating characters. It's only incidentally about the clothes.

As a child, I loved fashion. I enjoyed wearing clothes and making them, was good at art and devoured my mum's copies of *Nova* magazine, but somehow it never occurred to me to be a fashion designer. Perhaps it was simply too remote. Then, when I was a teenager growing up in London in the 1970s, I started going to the theatre and to a lot of dance performances. It was a wonderful time for interesting theatre and offbeat shows and there wasn't such a divide between the creators and the audience. It was all small-scale and open to new ideas. I loved the energy and the creativity. My interests in fashion and performance came together quite naturally.

One night when I was sixteen I met Lindsay Kemp, the radical choreographer. I just went up and introduced myself after a show. Working with him, and then later with Derek Jarman, confirmed that I didn't want to design pretty things for an anonymous person but specific clothes, maybe ugly, or worn-out or ill-fitting clothes, that told a narrative. I wanted to make costume for a performer — the clothes that would help them to create a character. I still enjoy that challenge, nearly fifty years later.

When I'm designing a look for a film or a play, I consult the writer and the script. Is it a period piece? Is it realism or is there an element of whimsy, fantasy? Is it a heightened aesthetic? I do my research and I hunt, like a magpie, for images that catch my eye. It's very intuitive. I don't work backwards from a meaning that I'm trying to convey. It's more a question of sensing when something looks and feels right. I think that's experience. You know when to stop with a look; you know when you've got it. Where appropriate, I like to combine elements in unexpected ways. A decorative detail that might be a little anachronistic but conveys the emotions of the character. But until the film or play is cast, I can't really start.

The biggest factor in my design of an individual character's costume is always what the actor brings. Their physicality. It is their job to embody the character and my job to give them tools to do so. Design happens in the fitting room, not on paper. It happens when you're messing with proportion, say. Maybe this character's trousers are too short and they haven't noticed. Or the waistband is a little tight but they haven't been able to afford a new suit for years.

The world of costume can feel very remote from everyday life, especially when it's costumes for a Hollywood film, but many of us dress in certain ways to tell the world our story. We have costumes for the roles we play, whether that's an interview suit or a party dress. In the late 1980s when I was just starting to get big jobs, I had an interview outfit that always made me feel confident. It was a Jean Paul Gaultier black bomber jacket that I wore with black breeches. Some pieces are so powerful that they last for ever. I still wear that jacket, though I lost its companion, the version with a bright-red lining. That got stolen from a film shoot in Uzbekistan. I sometimes wonder about the character who's wearing it now.

For many years I wore black but now I wear a lot of colour, though I am not a maximalist. I like a restricted palette and to use different tones. I like colours to be coordinated; I can't do real mixed colour. There have been other shifts, too. I used to wear gowns at big events and now wear suits, though I have always been comfortable wearing trousers and I wear them all the time at home. My personal style has evolved but there are some key elements that stay the same. I pay a lot of attention to proportion. **I don't really accessorise and my looks are always unfussy. The effect I aim to create is a powerful one.** And I don't follow trends because I know what suits me. I'm still wearing the same shapes I wore in the 1990s.

In the autumn of 2022, I had to plan an outfit in which to receive the BAFTA fellowship, a sort of lifetime achievement award. I knew I would be up on stage and would be photographed a lot. I'm not a performer, I work behind the scenes, so I was a little daunted. It helped to approach it as if it were a job. I wanted a suit but wasn't clear on much beyond that until, in October, I received an email from a young designer in New York called Hannah Soukup. She had made some trousers and she thought I might like them. We had met some years previously when I chased her down a street in Brooklyn to ask her where she got an amazing piece of sculptural knitwear that she was wearing. It turned out that she had made it. I bought a sweater and a scarf from her that day and we've been in touch ever since.

Hannah was right; I loved her design for the trousers, which were made from a black foam-backed wool, so soft and light, like a neoprene. They were balloon legged with a beautiful rippling-wave silhouette. I had Ian Frazer Wallace, my regular tailor, make me a jacket in the same fabric, inspired by an Alaïa bolero jacket from the 1980s. I had a new shirt made. Then I set about hunting for the shoes. I thought initially that it needed to be boot but in the end I wore shoes by Stella McCartney. I wanted to do my hair in a bright-orange Mr Whippy swirl, with the rippling edges echoing the outline of the trousers. Honestly, that outfit was like doing a whole production. I obsessed about every detail, and of course it all took longer than I thought it would and there were hitches and hold-ups. That's life. I did worry that I looked as if I was in fancy dress but, in the end, it was good. It was a little irreverent, which is what I wanted.

I'm not sure you can be stylish without being prepared to work for it, at least a bit. It's about paying attention, to what you're wearing and what's going on around you in the world. I think you're either interested in that visual culture or you're not. Sometimes people who have no desire to look 'fashion-y' still have a readily identifiable look. You spot your friend in a crowd, for example, because of that slouchy coat as well as the way they walk. I could create a costume for them if they were a character in a play. So that person might not be stylish as such; they might not be making conscious choices about what they wear, but they're still wearing clothes that make them look like themselves.

Style is about confidence. It's wanting to look a little bit different, it's wanting to stand out. You can't be stylish if you look like everyone else. You can perhaps be chic but even then . . . there's always something special that emanates. Perhaps a person is wearing a simple T-shirt and a blazer, but something's going on. Style is what's on the inside, really, which comes back to character. Dress for your character; embody it with your clothes, whoever you are.

The first piece I bought with my own money:

Back in the 1970s there was a shop called Bus Stop and there was a branch in Croydon, near where I grew up. When I was about eleven, I bought a pair of red tights there. I loved strong colour even then. And then later, I used to shoplift make-up and ostrich feathers from Biba. Everyone did. One feather at a time, to decorate my bedroom. I loved that whole thing: the 1970s doing the 1930s. If I were to wear a gown now it would be an early or late thirties piece. That's probably my favourite period.

The one piece I'd save if my home was on fire:

The first suit I wore to a red carpet event. It was made for me by my tailor, Ian, and inspired by Bowie's satin turquoise suit in the video for his song 'Life on Mars'. It was my homage to Bowie, who had died just a month previously and was also a Croydon-dwelling costume fanatic. He, like Biba, has been a huge influence. Perhaps it's the same for most of us: **the things we loved between the ages of twelve and sixteen leave indelible marks on ourselves and our style.**

ROBERT HARRIS
on Symbolism

Robert Harris is the bestselling author of fifteen novels, including *Fatherland*, the Cicero Trilogy and *Act of Oblivion*. In *Conclave*, 118 cardinals gather from around the world. Behind the locked doors of the Sistine Chapel, they are tasked with the election of a new Pope.

IT WAS JUST BEFORE 2 p.m. when Lomeli finally roused himself from his bed. He undressed to his underwear and socks, opened his closet and laid out the various elements of his choir dress on the counterpane. As he removed each item from its cellophane wrapping, it exuded the sweet chemical aroma of dry-cleaning fluid – a scent that always reminded him of his years in the Nuncio's residence in New York, when all his laundry was done at a place on East 72nd Street. For a moment he closed his eyes and heard once more the ceaseless soft horns of the distant Manhattan traffic.

Every garment had been made to measure by Gammarelli, papal outfitters since 1798, in their famous shop behind the Pantheon, and **he took his time in dressing, meditating on the sacred nature of each element in an effort to heighten his spiritual awareness.**

He slipped his arms into the scarlet woollen cassock and fastened the thirty-three buttons that ran from his neck to his ankles – one button for each year of Christ's life. Around his waist he tied the red watered-silk sash of the cincture, or fascia, designed to remind him of his vow of chastity, and checked to make sure its tasselled end hung to a point midway up his left calf. Then he pulled over his head the thin white linen rochet

— the symbol, along with the mozzetta, of his judicial authority. The bottom two-thirds and the cuffs were of white lace with a floral pattern. He tied the tapes in a bow at his neck and tugged the rochet down so that it extended to just below his knees. Finally he put on his mozzetta, an elbow-length nine-buttoned scarlet cape.

He picked up his pectoral cross from the nightstand and kissed it. John Paul II had presented him in person with the cross to mark his recall from New York to Rome to serve as Secretary for Relations with Foreign States. The Pope's Parkinsonism had been terribly advanced by then; his hands had shaken so much as he tried to hand it over, it had dropped on the floor. Lomeli unclipped the gold chain and replaced it with a cord of red and gold silk. He murmured the customary prayer for protection (*Munire digneris me . . .*) and hung the cross round his neck so that it lay next to his heart. Then he sat on the edge of the bed, worked his feet into a pair of well-worn black leather brogues and tied the laces. Only one item remained: his biretta of scarlet silk, which he placed over his skullcap.

On the back of the bathroom door was a full-length mirror. He switched on the stuttering light and checked himself in the bluish glow: front first, then his left side, then his right. His profile had become beaky with age. He thought he looked like some elderly moulting bird. Sister Anjelica, who kept house for him, was always telling him he was too thin, that he should eat more. Hanging up in his apartment were vestments he had first worn as a young priest more than forty years ago and which still fitted him perfectly. He smoothed his hands over his stomach. He felt hungry. He has missed both breakfast and lunch. Let it be so, he thought. The pangs of hunger would serve as a useful mortification of the flesh, a constant tiny reminder throughout the first round of voting of the vast agony of Christ's sacrifice.

JOAN COLLINS
on Making the Best of Oneself

Something of a living legend, Joan Collins, OBE has appeared in numerous films and television series, most famously as Alexis Carrington Colby in the hit TV drama *Dynasty*. In *The World According to Joan* she shares her life experience with her trademark wit and wisdom.

IN 1955 I HAD JUST been cast in my first Hollywood movie, *The Girl in the Red Velvet Swing*. The part had been intended for Marilyn Monroe, but when she left Fox, fed up with the studio system, the role fell to me. At the age of twenty-one I was to play the most beautiful girl in New York.

After a day of rehearsing I walked into the cafeteria on the Fox studio lot for lunch wearing blue jeans, and a T-shirt – and believe it or not – not a scrap of make-up.

As I walked through the café towards Richard Fleischer, the director of my movie, he saw me and threw his hands in the air.

'Oh my God,' he said, 'I can't look at you. You look hideous. You should always appear in public with full make-up, a nice dress and white gloves, otherwise you'll never get anywhere in this business.'

So I decided I better start smartening up my act.

My mother and my nine aunts were incredibly glamorous. They wouldn't have dreamed of stepping outside the house without wearing make-up and with their hair beautifully done. But then the forties and fifties were incredibly glamorous decades. Women looked up to film stars such as Hedy Lamarr, Betty Grable and Joan Crawford (after whom I am named). The clothes these

211

stars wore on screen were often more important than the films themselves. So many women could sew then, and the films were like catwalks of fashion that they could replicate.

From the twenties to the sixties, ordinary women tried their best to look like their favourite stars. My mother aspired to Greer Garson and my Aunt Lalla to Marlene Dietrich. Then everything changed in the grungy seventies, before glamour made a big comeback in the eighties.

By then I had gained a reputation as a woman who always made the best of herself. When I made *The Stud* and then *The Bitch* in the late seventies, **I invented a look which I've stuck to more or less ever since:** big hair, smoky eyes and bright lipstick. So, when *Dynasty* and Alexis Carrington came along, her look was already in place — it was mine.

Yves Saint Laurent and Pierre Cardin had just launched the big shoulder-padded look on the fashion world, and that felt right for Alexis. My dear friend Nolan Miller, the designer on the show, agreed that Alexis was a woman of the world, totally familiar with haute couture, so Nolan and I worked together and would go to the department stores Saks and Neiman Marcus every Saturday to pull designer clothes off the rails that we thought were very Alexis.

When I catch the odd photo of myself or other stars of eighties' TV, I'm often impressed by how good we all looked: groomed and well put together and frankly, m'dear, everyone unique, with their own style of hair and clothing. There I am posed on the steps of Alexis' Gulf Stream, wearing a pale grey jersey dress with a sweetheart neckline, accentuated with diamond clips, a matching cloche turban and gloves, enveloped by a grey cashmere cape edged in grey fox. Or posing with the other stars of *Dynasty*, all impossibly tiny-waisted, I'm in a gold lame sleeveless, backless and almost frontless evening gown, also split to the thigh.

No-one is born glamorous but practically anyone can develop glamour.

CHIMAMANDA NGOZI ADICHIE
on Making the Right Impression

Born in Nigeria in 1977, Chimamanda is a prize-winning author. This piece first appeared in US *Elle*.

AS A CHILD, I LOVED watching my mother get dressed for Mass. She folded and twisted and pinned her ichafu until it sat on her head like a large flower. She wrapped her George — heavy beaded cloth, alive with embroidery, always in bright shades of red or purple or pink — around her waist in two layers. The first, the longer piece, hit her ankles, and the second formed an elegant tier just below her knees. Her sequined blouse caught the light and glittered. Her shoes and handbag always matched. Her lips shone with gloss. As she moved, so did the heady scent of Dior Poison. I loved, too, the way she dressed me in pretty little-girl clothes, lace-edged socks pulled up to my calves, my hair arranged in two puffy bunny-tails. My favorite memory is of a sunny Sunday morning, standing in front of her dressing table, my mother clasping her necklace around my neck, a delicate gold wisp with a fish-shape pendant, the mouth of the fish open as though in delighted surprise.

For her work as a university administrator, my mother also wore color: skirt suits, feminine swingy dresses belted at the waist, medium-high heels. She was stylish, but she was not unusual. Other middle-class Igbo women also invested in gold jewelry, in good shoes, in appearance. They searched for the best tailors to make clothes for them and their children. If they were lucky enough to travel abroad, they shopped mostly for clothes and shoes. They spoke of grooming almost in moral terms. The rare woman who did not appear well dressed and well lotioned was frowned upon, as though her appearance were a character failing. 'She doesn't look like a person,' my mother would say.

As a teenager, I searched her trunks for crochet tops from the 1970s. I took a pair of her old jeans to a seamstress who turned them into a miniskirt. I once wore my brother's tie, knotted like a man's, to a party. For my 17th birthday, I designed a halter maxidress, low in the back, the collar lined with plastic pearls. My tailor, a gentle man sitting in his market stall, looked baffled while I explained it to him. My mother did not always approve of these clothing choices, but what mattered to her was that I made an effort. Ours was a relatively privileged life, but to pay attention to appearance − and to look as though one did − was a trait that cut across class in Nigeria.

When I left home to attend university in America, the insistent casualness of dress alarmed me. I was used to a casualness with care − T-shirts ironed crisp, jeans altered for the best fit − but it seemed that these students had rolled out of bed in their pajamas and come straight to class. Summer shorts were so short they seemed like underwear, and how, I wondered, could people wear rubber flip-flops to school?

Still, I realized quickly that some outfits I might have casually worn on a Nigerian university campus would simply be impossible now. I made slight amendments to accommodate my new American life. A lover of dresses and skirts, I began to wear more jeans. I walked more often in America, so I wore fewer high heels, but always made sure my flats were feminine. I refused to wear sneakers outside a gym. Once, an American friend told me, 'You're over-dressed.' In my short-sleeve top, cotton trousers, and high wedge sandals, I did see her point, especially for an undergraduate class. But I was not uncomfortable. I felt like myself.

My writing life changed that. Short stories I had been working on for years were finally receiving nice, handwritten rejection notes. This was progress of sorts. Once, at a workshop, I sat with other unpublished writers, silently nursing our hopes and watching the faculty — published writers who seemed to float in their accomplishment. A fellow aspiring writer said of one faculty member, 'Look at that dress and make-up! You can't take her seriously.' I thought the woman looked attractive, and I admired the grace with which she walked in her heels. But I found myself quickly agreeing. Yes, indeed, one could not take this author of three novels seriously, because she wore a pretty dress and two shades of eye shadow.

I had learned a lesson about Western culture: Women who wanted to be taken seriously were supposed to substantiate their seriousness with a studied indifference to appearance. For serious women writers in particular, it was better not to dress well at all, and if you did, then it was best to pretend that you had not put much thought into it. If you spoke of fashion, it had to be either with apology or with the slightest of sneers. The further your choices were from the mainstream, the better. The only circumstance under which caring about clothes was acceptable was when making a statement, creating an image of some sort to be edgy, eclectic, counterculture. It could not merely be about taking pleasure in clothes.

A good publisher had bought my novel. I was twenty-six years old. I was eager to be taken seriously. And so began my years of pretense. I hid my high heels. I told myself that orange, flattering to my skin tone, was too loud. That my large earrings were too much. I wore clothes I would ordinarily consider uninteresting, nothing too bright or too fitted or too unusual. I made choices thinking only about this: How should a serious woman writer be? I didn't want to look as if I tried too hard. I also wanted to look older. Young and female seemed to me a bad combination for being taken seriously.

Once, I brought a pair of high heels to a literary event but left them in my suitcase and wore flats instead. An old friend said, 'Wear what you want to; it's your work that matters.' But he was a man, and I thought that was easy for him to say.

Intellectually, I agreed with him. I would have said the same thing to someone else. But it took years before I truly began to believe this.

During the book tour for *Americanah* I wore, for the first time, clothes that made me happy. My favorite outfit was a pair of ankara-print shorts, a damask top, and yellow high-heel shoes. Perhaps it is the confidence that comes with being older. **Perhaps it is the good fortune of being published and read seriously, but I no longer pretend not to care about clothes. Because I do care. I love embroidery and texture. I love lace and full skirts and cinched waists. I love black, and I love color. I love heels, and I love flats. I love exquisite detailing. I love shorts and long maxidresses and feminine jackets with puffy sleeves. I love colored trousers. I love shopping. I love my two wonderful tailors in Nigeria, who often give me suggestions and with whom I exchange sketches.** I admire well-dressed women and often make a point to tell them so. Just because I dress now thinking of what I like, what I think fits and flatters, what puts me in a good mood. I feel again myself — an idea that is no less true for being a bit hackneyed.

I like to think of this, a little fancifully, as going back to my roots. I grew up, after all, in a world in which a woman's seriousness was not incompatible with an interest in appearance; if anything, an interest in appearance was expected of women who wanted to be taken seriously.

My mother made history as the first woman to be registrar of the University of Nigeria at Nsukka; her speeches at senate meetings were famous for their eloquence and brilliance. Now, at seventy, she still loves clothes. Our tastes, though, are very different. She wishes I were more conventional. She would like to see me wearing jewelry that matches and long hair weaves. (In her world, better one real-gold set than twenty of what she calls 'costume'; in her world, my kinky hair is 'untidy.') Still, I am my mother's daughter, and I invest in appearance.

ÉMILE ZOLA
on Paradisical Abundance

The Ladies' Paradise is the eleventh in Zola's twenty-novel series, *Les Rougon-Macquart*. Zola was politically active, famously publishing *J'Accuse . . .!*, an open letter which condemned the French army for being antisemitic and wrongfully convicting Alfred Dreyfus of treason. This novel, published in 1883, was a response to the class conflicts dividing France in the mid-nineteenth century.

ON EACH SIDE OF THE heavy columns were draped with cloth, making the background appear still more distant. **And the dresses were in this sort of chapel raised to the worship of woman's beauty and grace. Occupying the centre was a magnificent article, a velvet mantle, trimmed with silver fox;** on one side a silk cape lined with miniver, on the other a cloth cloak edged with cocks' 'plumes'; and last of all, opera cloaks in white cashmere and white silk trimmed with swansdown or chenille. There was something for all tastes, from the opera clocks at twenty-nine francs to the velvet mantle marked up at eighteen hundred. The well-rounded neck and graceful figures of the dummeries exaggerated the slimness of the waist. The absent head being replaced by a large price-ticket pinned on the neck; whilst the mirrors, cleverly arranged on each side of the window, reflected and amidst a complication of ornaments covered with gilding. Two allegorical figures, representing two laughing, bare-breasted women, unrolled the scroll bearing the sign, 'The Ladies' Paradise'. The establishment extended along the Rue de la Michodiere and the Rue Neuve-Saint-Augustin and comprises, beside the corner

217

house, four others – two on the right and two on the left, bought and fitted up recently. It seemed to her an endless extension, with its display on the ground floor, and the plate-glass windows, through which could be seen the whole length of the counters. Upstairs a young lady, dressed all in silk, was sharpening a pencil, while two others, beside her, were unfolding some velvet mantles.

'The Ladies' Paradise,' read Jean, with the tender laugh of a handsome youth who had already had an adventure with a woman. 'That must draw the customers – eh?'

But Denise was absorbed by the display at the principal entrance. There she saw, in the open street, on the very pavement, **a mountain of cheap goods – bargains, placed there to tempt the passers-by, and attract attention.** Hanging from above were pieces of woollen and cloth goods, merinos, cheviots, and tweeds, floating like flags; the neutral, slate, navy-blue, and olive-green tints being relieved by the large white price-tickets. Close by, round the doorway, were hanging strips of fur, narrow bands for dress trimmings, fine Siberian squirrel-skin, spotless snowy swansdown, rabbit-skin imitation ermine and imitation sable. Below, on shelves and on tables, amidst a pile of remnants, appeared an immense quality of hosiery, almost given away knitted woollen gloves, neckerchiefs, women's hoods, waistcoats, a winter show in all colors, striped, dyed, and variegated, with here and there a flaming patch of red. Denise saw some tartan at nine sous, some strips of American vision at a franc, and some mittens at five sous. There appeared to be an immense clearance sale going on; the establishment seemed bursting with goods, blocking up the pavement with the surplus.

JARVIS COCKER
on Jumble Sales

With a penchant for velvet jackets and charity-shop shirts, the charismatic front man and lyricist of Pulp has always had a strong sense of style. This is an extract from his memoir *Good Pop, Bad Pop*, a look at the objects he found in his loft and what this collection of broken glasses and souvenirs say about him.

I'M NOW HOLDING A SHIRT. It's orange with white circles on it. 'Prova' is embroidered on the label. I think that was the home brand of British Home Stores.

This is a 'Gold Star' shirt. That might have had something to do with why I bought it. More positive visualisation. But the main reason I'm showing you this is that, as far as I remember (fanfare, please), this is the first second-hand clothing I ever bought.

That was a big step for me. I got into buying second-hand clothes because just one hundred yards away from the family home was a Methodist church, & they had jumble sales in their church hall from time to time. & my discovery of jumble sales pretty much coincided with my discovery of punk.

The nearest thing to jumble sales in the present day are car boot sales, but the atmosphere is substantially different at a car boot sale. At jumble sales people donate their unwanted items so they can be re-sold to raise money for a new church roof or whatever. At a car boot sale the sellers are hoping to personally benefit from selling their items. The philanthropic element is absent. Plus, programmes such as *Antiques Roadshow* have made customers think that they might stumble across a priceless master-piece they can sell on at auction for millions. So the atmosphere

219

can be a little 'charged'. I remember once seeing a guy at a car boot sale turn over a vase so that he could look at the maker's mark on the bottom – he must have seen an expert do that on telly – & all this slop that looked like a discarded Pot Noodle slid out of the vase & down his sleeve. That kind of sums up car boot sales for me.

Jumble sales were much mellower. & they were such a source of inspiration to my younger self. The message taken from punk was that 'it's OK to look different'. I was no longer going to try (& fail) to fit in – so from now on I was going to buy my own clothes. The only problem with this resolution was that I didn't actually have any money. I mean, I *was* doing a paper round. So I was earning maybe £2 a week. But, even allowing for inflation, I think you can tell that wasn't going to go very far in funding my Extreme Makeover.

So jumble sales really were a godsend. They were cheap. Incredibly cheap, really. You generally had to pay 5p to get in, & then individual items would be somewhere between 10 & 20p each. Affordable. You could get a whole new wardrobe for under a pound. & because the clothes were so cheap you could really experiment. Take a leap in the dark. You could see something & think, 'Well, it's only 10p, so I'll buy it & see what it looks like when I get home. Maybe a batwing jumper will really suit me.'

Jumble sales were also where I discovered my hunter-gatherer instinct. You had to dive into these big piles of clothing along with everyone else & just rummage around until you found something that took your fancy. It could get pretty physical. You had to think fast if you didn't want to leave empty-handed. Steep learning curve for a shy teenager.

It certainly beat going to a regular shop – apart from the price aspect, I'd never particularly liked going to shops anyway, especially clothes shops – because the assistants would invariably want to talk to you & sometimes even follow you around the shop when all you wanted to do was browse in peace. Plus, normal shops now seemed boring in comparison to jumble sales. Everything just hanging there meekly on a clothes rail. You didn't have to fight a gang of old women to get to what you wanted. Pretty tame.

& where were the refreshments? Tea was available at a very reasonable price at a jumble sale. & home-made cake. It was a scene. A complete day out. For a quid or so.

So, I'm glad I still have this. The first shirt that I ever bought from a jumble sale. It contravenes the Shirt Rule as featured in the Pulp Manifesto: 'plain-coloured shirts (no patterns)' (told you that rule didn't last very long), but that doesn't matter, it marks the dawn of a new sensibility.

Because as well as getting myself something to wear, I was also now taking society's cast-offs & 're-purposing' them. I was learning about the world by looking at what it threw away. By what it deemed 'worthless'. **This was the real beginning of the Pulp aesthetic. Sifting through the debris to find an alternative to the official narrative.** Using second-hand items to tell a brand-new story.

To tell my own story. Which is pretty much the definition of the creative act, as far as I can make out.

FIONA STUART
on Vintage Discoveries

Fiona opened Rellik, one of London's best-loved vintage fashion stores, with two friends back in 1999. Over the course of her thirty-year career buying and selling second-hand designer fashion, she's come across many treasures and been at the forefront of the sector as it transformed from niche to mainstream. She's learned that you will never go wrong if you buy Celine, Yves Saint Laurent, 1980s Alaïa or Ungaro, Helmut Lang, Margiela or Versace.

FOR ME, THE TERM 'VINTAGE' refers to a piece that can hold its value. We used to think of vintage fashion as being from a certain period, and at least twenty years old. I think that's changed. Nowadays, vintage might be relatively recent but it has a value that's going to grow over time. Sometimes that value is clear right from a piece's first appearance. In other cases, it only becomes evident over time, and often much later. Think of the early Queen shows – Freddie Mercury's clothes were relevant, trendsetting, valuable right from the moment he wore them. The other end of the spectrum might be Paul Poiret's pleated draped gowns from the 1910s, which caused huge debate at the time and were as hated as they were feted but became the template for a new way to dress. The judgment call about value in fashion can be hard to make, of course, but over the years I've developed my instincts.

I had no idea there was such a thing as vintage style until I arrived in London. I grew up partly in Australia, where fashion felt quite distant and we made our own clothes from patterns, but also in Singapore where there was a lot of influence from US pop culture. I remember disco being huge there. When I was about twelve years old, I started to feel the hunger that grips you when you decide you absolutely *need* a certain fashion item. The first obsession I recall was a pair of high-heeled zip-up brown leather boots that I'd seen on TV. I remember dragging my poor grandmother all over the mall until I found something similar.

I don't think I've ever stopped being excited by that quest for the perfect, transformational piece. That's the great pleasure of vintage fashion, for me: the discovery. Even more than actually wearing what you find. My first big discovery was a Pucci silk shirt in an Oxfam shop in Colindale. I didn't know anything about Pucci but I knew I liked the shirt. It was the late 1980s and by then I was living near the Portobello Market and I used to go shopping for bargains every week. After a while I realised that you could sell as well as buy, so I sold that shirt to a stall holder, who definitely did know about Pucci, and knew exactly how much it was worth!

As well as the treasure hunt aspect, the other thing I love is the process of learning about what you find. **So many times I've picked up something that appeals to me and then started doing research and ended up diving down rabbit holes into the history of Belle Epoque Paris or New York in the 1970s. I once found a dress made in the Charles Worth factory that sent me off into a world I hadn't known anything about.** You figure out why you love something or why it has a value by learning about its place in history. Sometimes that happens in a library – though these days it's all online, of course – but sometimes you plug into the history through the transaction of buying and the conversation with the seller. I remember going to a car boot sale and meeting a woman who was selling loads of 1930s chiffon tea dresses. She told me that her grandfather had owned a clothing factory, and these had been her grandmother's dresses. If something interests me, I get excited; I want to know more. If you're a bit obsessive, as I am, it can become a way of life.

When I started, I used to wear everything I bought. Before we opened Rellik I had a stall on Portobello Market. When I got hold of those 1930s dresses I wore them all on rotation, I loved them. I didn't wear the Christian Dior wedding dress I found at a car boot sale but I wore pretty much everything else. As I've got older, my taste has become simpler. Currently, my favourite thing in my wardrobe is a Yohji Yamamoto jumpsuit, which feels heavenly on. It's so comfortable; I absolutely love it and wouldn't sell it. I had a couple of Ossie Clark dresses, on the other hand, and yes they were beautiful but having worn them once I knew I wouldn't wear them again. They got sold. I think being a dealer makes you less hung up on owning things.

It's not as simple as having money. I've been invited to sell pieces by very wealthy people whose taste didn't run to clothes that would prove their value over time. I've also come across countless people who didn't have a lot of money but whose nose for pieces of enduring interest and appeal was absolutely spot on.

I meet a lot of people who are obsessed with clothes, many of whom are very stylish. When they come into the shop some of them are very experienced and used to following their instincts, some are trainspotters searching for a particular piece, some are just getting into second-hand and vintage and are curious and exploring. In every case, what makes them stylish is their ability to really wear the clothes, rather than have the clothes wear them. **Great vintage clothes-wearers are not following a look book, they're wearing a 1940s dress with a 1970s belt and some new trainers, say.** They have the gift for mixing it up.

It's so much easier to educate yourself about fashion and style now, which is brilliant but of course also means it's much harder to find great stuff in charity shops, say. But there are wonderful pieces out there and there will always be a designer you don't yet know about, waiting to be discovered. I still find clothes thrilling but I know that one day, after I'm dead and gone, someone will go through my things looking for pieces they can sell on. That's all part of the cycle, in life and fashion.

SOPHIE DAHL
on Scent

A writer and scent aficionado who wrote a regular column on perfume for *Vogue*, this piece on the language of flowers first appeared in *Harper's Bazaar*.

MY FRIENDS AND I USED to braid it into our hair when we were young teenagers, spending monsoon summers with our spiritually restless mothers in an ashram in India, high up in the green mountains of the Maharashtra State.

In India, as night fell, the bats swept low and we scattered across the dusty road away from them, shrieking and laughing. They kept coming, dive bombing down, close enough for the movement of their wings to stir our hair, drawn in by the siren call of the white flowers crowning it.

For me, the scent of tuberose is awakening, paired with incense and mysticism. It spells warm rain pounding against the silk of a bandage-tight choli, dyeing the skin underneath a violent pink. Memories of chanting in a darkened room papered with peacock feathers. Losing sight of the world in the flames of a bonfire that was meant to burn away all earthly sin as we danced around it, a band of lost, devout, fragrant girls.

That sharp, narcotic reek, at first godly, became in later adolescence, the smell of seduction. Glamorous mothers, my mother, the card-carrying alphas of super-femininity, always seemed to enter a room in a cloud of Guerlain's Après L'Ondée, or Robert Piguet's Fracas. I was allowed to wear a whisper of the latter behind the ears to my first dance, along with sticky lip-gloss and mascara. I remember dragging the cool edge of the glass stopper behind my schoolgirl bob, not yet understanding the full scope

225

of its buttery, carnal power. **I knew enough to recognise that it was a symbol though, some initiation into womanhood.**

The late stylist Isabella Blow, who was to enter and change my life like a maverick locomotive when I was eighteen, always wore some variation of tuberose. I was a stranger sitting on her doorstep, crying, when she stepped out of a cab in a cloud of it, wearing a galleon ship upon her head. I wonder now if the familiarity of her smell contributed to how at home I felt with her? On her ivory skin, the flower continued an elusive trajectory, spilling off McQueen jackets and stockings from Chantal Thomas, the scraps of lace from fleamarkets in Paris that trailed from her Globe-Trotter suitcases in a compelling stream. She wore powdery tuberoses, L'Artisan Parfumeur's was one, and along with her Mr Pearl corsets, slash of red lipstick, honk of a laugh and Philip Treacy hats, the scent was her daemon. To smell it now would be to throw me, Alice down the rabbit hole, into a time in which I played dress up with grown-ups, sharing laughs and cigarettes in their kitchens, ignorant of the fact that many of them would not make it through. When you're young, it feels like everyone will live forever. Tuberose is also the smell of loss, of disbelief and grey days, churches and funeral hats.

My grandmother wore Chanel 5, as she called it, forever her old faithful, and I wore and wear Fracas the same, though I mix it up, playing with others like some ingénue alchemist. Tammy Frazer's Rose and Tuberose is a lovely splashy green thing; Katharine Hepburn would have worn it had it been around when she was, in all her golf-playing, tweedy glory. And then there is the wonderfully virginal Estée Lauder Private Collection Tuberose Gardenia, which is like the sweetest linen, sheets. For the less chaste, there is Serge Lutens' Tubéreuse Criminelle, a complicated scent that begins with the mentholated medicinal and ends on something pure and creamy; or Frédéric Malle's Carnal Flower, again, a chameleon, an almost caffeinated kick that

undresses to white flowers within a few minutes and is unflinch-
ingly sexy.

Although I'm a scent junkie, and revel in the discovery of
something new and exciting, whilst still hankering for the classics (Mitsouko, Calèche, Rive Gauche), nothing for me packs
the same erotic punch as Fracas or a real-life cluster of tuberose
itself, I suppose, because both are so wrapped up in the olfactory
memory bank of firsts. Fervours, friendships, dances, kisses,
losses, loves: tuberose has been the base note to my life, whether
in a temple, train, school run, or a hip hop night at Don Hills,
twenty-five years ago. It's potent and punchy. It has a message,
as my friend Bay would say.

DOROTHY PARKER
on the Satin Dress

Dorothy Parker (1893–1967) was a poet and regular at
New York's Algonquin Hotel in the 1920s.

NEEDLE, needle, dip and dart,
Thrusting up and down,
Where's the man could ease a heart
Like a satin gown?

See the stitches curve and crawl
Round the cunning seams—
Patterns thin and sweet and small
As a lady's dreams.

Wantons go in bright brocades;
Brides in organdie;
Gingham's for the plighted maid;
Satin's for the free!

Wool's to line a miser's chest;
Crape's to calm the old;
Velvet hides an empty breast;
Satin's for the bold!

Lawn is for a bishop's yoke;
Linen's for a nun;
Satin is for wiser folk—
Would the dress were done!

Satin glows in candle-light—
Satin's for the proud!
They will say who watch at night,
'What a fine shroud!'

ACKNOWLEDGEMENTS

THANK YOU, TOM CRAIG — hands down the most stylish man I know. And thank you to my children, Billy and Sylvie — you are THE BEST. To my sisters, Rose and Daisy — both brilliant and inspiring.

Thank you to my brilliant editor, Jocasta Hamilton, who came swooping into my life and made everything look so easy and inspiring, and without whom this book would not exist — in every single way. And to Helen Coyle, the best co-worker/ writer on this project I could have dreamed of. And to Charlotte Robathan — for being so smart and meticulous.

Special thanks to the women in my life who have been SO inspiring around clothes in so many different ways to me. In particular:

To Kira Jolliffe for everything. There's too much to mention, but especially for being the best partner in crime when it came to clothes. I learnt so much from you.

To Sarah Hiscox for having the best taste, listening to me and encouraging me about this book (and everything else) and for being such a wonderful friend.

To Charlotte Tilbury for always wanting her friends to be the best possible version of themselves — in all ways. And for always making me want to look my best, and throw on a belt, a bag, a lash . . .

To Chloë Sevigny for just being a genius with clothes and style, for being so inspiring, and for her continued support and loyalty in being part of projects that I work on. Thank you, Chloë!

To Anita Pallenberg, who brought so much style, richness, inspiration, independence and rock 'n' roll spirit into my life.

To the unforgettable Stella Tennant — style and beauty in spades.

To Alannah Weston for her support and encouragement around me and my passion for second-hand clothes.

And to Emma Fabien at Oxfam – for all the fun and excitement whilst working together on the Fashion Fighting Poverty shows, Second Hand September and the other projects around clothes which are becoming a powerful force for activism.

Thank you, Alexandra Shulman, for being so supportive.

Thank you to all the contributors for your generosity and insight.

And thank you to all my friends – almost all of whom I have spent many mornings at the market or thrift store with.

TEXT PERMISSIONS

Page 7: © Bernardine Evaristo, 2023; Page 10: Transcribed extracts from 'The David Bowie Story' BBC Radio One, 1993; Page 15: Extracts from *Orlando* (1928) by Virginia Woolf; Page 16: Extracts from *Life as a Unicorn* reprinted by permission of HarperCollins Publishers Ltd, © 2019 Amrou Al-Kadhi; Page 18: 'Upon Julia's Clothes' (1648) by Robert Herrick; Page 19: From *The Cost of Living* by Deborah Levy published by Penguin. Copyright © Deborah Levy, 2018. Reprinted by permission of Penguin Books Limited; Page 21: Extracts from manifesto for The Rational Dress Society, 1881 and from the catalogue of their inaugural exhibition, 1883; Page 31: From *Foxy* by Pam Grier, copyright © 2010. Reprinted by permission of Grand Central Publishing, an imprint of Hachette Book Group, Inc; Page 49: Extract from *Claudine At School* by Colette published by Vintage Classics. Copyright © Colette, 1900. Reprinted by permission of Penguin Books Limited; Page 50: Extract from *Anna Karenina* (1877) by Leo Tolstoy; Page 52: © Stanley Tucci, 2023; Page 54: Extract from *On Human Finery*. Reprinted by permission of The Society of Authors, © 1947 Quentin Bell; Page 55: Extract from *No Name in the Street* (1972) by James Baldwin; Page 56: Extract from an interview with Fran Lebowitz for *Elle* US, © Kathleen Hale, 2015; Page 58: Extract from *The White Album*. Reprinted by permission of HarperCollins Publishers Ltd, © 2017 Joan Didion; Page 60: © Zadie Smith 2019; Page 67: Extract from 'The Philosophy of Dress' by Oscar Wilde. Originally published in the *New-York Tribune* 1885; Page 97: Extract from *Dandy in the Underworld* (2003) by Sebastian Horsley published by Sceptre. Reprinted by permission of Hodder & Stoughton Ltd; Page 102: Extracts from *The Painter of Modern Life* (1863) by Charles Baudelaire; Page 113: Reprinted by permission of Young Kim, © Malcolm

McLaren; Page 121: Extract from *Dracula* (1897) by Bram Stoker; Page 128: From *Grace* by Grace Coddington published by Chatto & Windus. Copyright © Grace Coddington, 2012. Reprinted by permission of The Random House Group Limited; Page 135: Extract from *The Red Shoes* (1845) by Hans Christian Andersen; Page 141: Extract from *I Know Why the Caged Bird Sings*. Reprinted by permission of Little, Brown Book Group, © 1969 Maya Angelou; Page 146: Extracts from *Male and Female Costume: Grecian and Roman Costume, British Costume from the Roman Invasion Until 1822, and the Principles of Costume Applied to the Improved Dress of the Present Day* (1932) by Beau Brummell; Page 153: Extract from *The Great Gatsby* (1925) by F. Scott Fitzgerald; Page 161: Extract from *The Bell Jar*, 2010. Reprinted by permission of Faber, © Sylvia Plath; Page 166: Interview with Anita Pallenberg by Kira Jolliffe, reprinted by permission of *Cheap Date* magazine; Page 171: © Hanif Kureishi, 2023; Page 177: From *Polo* by Jilly Cooper published by Transworld POS. Copyright © Jilly Cooper, 1991. Reprinted by permission of The Random House Group Limited; Page 191: © Penelope Tree, 2023; Page 201: Extract from *Just Kids*, 2010. Reprinted by permission of Bloomsbury Publishing Plc, © Patti Smith; Page 203: Reprinted by permission of Tree Wright of the Anaïs Nin Literary Trust, © Anaïs Nin; Page 209: Extract from *Conclave* © Robert Harris 2016, published by Penguin Books Limited; Page 211: Extract from *The World According to Joan*, 2012. Reprinted by permission of Little, Brown Book Group, © Joan Collins; Page 213: Reprinted by permission of *Elle* US, © 2014 Chimamanda Ngozi Adichie; Page 217: Extract from *The Ladies' Paradise*, originally published as *Au Bonheur des Dames* (1883) by Émile Zola; Page 219: From *Good Pop, Bad Pop* by Jarvis Cocker published by Vintage. Copyright © Jarvis Cocker, 2022. Reprinted by permission of The Random House Group Limited; Page 225: © Sophie Dahl, 2023; Page 228: Extract from *Enough Rope* (1926) by Dorothy Parker.